# Understanding Media Theory

translated by Laura Martz

**V2_/NAi Publishers**

# Understanding Media Theory

## Arjen Mulder

Language, Image, Sound, Behavior

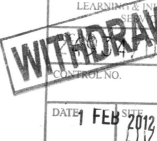

Preface

This is not a book about the best way to get into the media. Nor does it describe how, once you are in the media, you can most effectively profile yourself. It will not teach you how to best communicate your message, regardless of that message's social desirability. Nor is it about the temptations of the media or the dangers they pose to the individual, the family and society: violence, child porn, dumbing down, or manipulation of the masses. It is not an ode to media, nor is it a pessimistic look at the cultural decay alleged to be an inevitable consequence of ever-increasing media power. Finally, the book does not survey or detail the technical workings of media. It does not discuss circuits, relay stations, microchips, transistors or other mechanical and electronic components of media. Nor does it discuss goose quills, papyrus production or the secrets of oil paint.

This book is a theoretical introduction to media. It is about the new media as well as the old, many of which are still alive and kicking. This book describes how media make us who we are. It seeks to understand the media of the last hundred thousand years and learn to play with them instead of being played with by them. It seeks to create distance from what we become through our ongoing interaction with media. The media are repeatedly read in this book in terms of their technical capabilities and limitations, which can be seen in the capabilities and limitations of the worldview and emotional spectrum of the users of those media. All media are directed at our bodies. Media theory endeavors to discover how our bodies react to media and how they are programmed by media to react in a certain way. Media influence our bodies independently of our selves, whether we like it or not. Our bodies, however, do not exist independently of our selves, for who we are and what we are, are almost one and the same thing. Therefore media also determine in considerable part who we are.

This book comprises three parts plus an introduction. The first part, "General Media Theory," develops a theory which is applicable to every medium at once, whether binoculars, painting or hypertext – although the emphasis here is on visual media. The second part, "Historical Media Theory," describes how new media have been introduced again and again throughout history, and what their consequences have been for humans and society – this time with a focus on language media. The third part, "Practical Media Theory," describes how the media intervene in our lives on an everyday level, and how we can respond. The media of behavior and sound are also dealt with more extensively here. So-called "dead media," such as tom-toms and pneumatic dispatch, fall outside the scope of this book. The introduction, "Media Theory: The New Science," describes what media are and what media theory's origins and ultimate goals are.

Because the point of departure is always the question of what kinds of experiences media evoke in their users, no prior knowledge is needed to read this book other than an everyday familiarity with media, which is in any case characteristic of our age and our society. A certain openness with respect to art is necessary, for almost all the examples and applications of the theory discussed come from the artistic field. Art need not be discussed ponderously: no one knows what it is, and everyone must discover for themselves what it might be. In this book, art (literature, painting, photography, film, music, interactive installations, and so on) is considered to be a particular way of handling media and using them to call forth certain experiences. These experiences are linked to the canon of media theory books that have been published in the past sixty years, supplemented with a few precursors from previous centuries. At the moment, one theoretical introduction to new media after the other is being published, and rightly so, except that in these books the foundation for thinking about media is either left out or else mentioned in passing. And this is not right: "classical media theory" is much richer than any contemporary thought about contemporary media.

Media theory as it is taught in art schools, colleges and universities contains three main currents. The first emanates from film and television studies, and cultural studies with a focus on visual culture. The second springs from literary studies. These two currents can be easily separated on the basis of the various books' bibliographies, which always include or omit certain authors. An important third current is borne by artists producing machine art, interactive installations and network art, but also by non-university intellectuals who practice speculative media theory. All of them feel the hot breath of the media down their necks and can maintain their position only by developing their own, often very personal, theories about what media and technology can do. This current has remained largely invisible to academics, though almost all the big media theory discoveries have been made or sensed for the first time in this artistic domain. All of media theory, for that matter, springs from an artistic movement, namely twentieth-century Modernism, as will be made apparent in "Media Theory: The New Science."

Classical media theory consists of three schools which developed more or less independently of each other. In the first school, a central place is occupied by Marshall McLuhan (1911–1980).[1] He began in the 1930s as a literary scholar and in the 1950s developed into the first pure media theorist under the influence of communication historian Harold Innis. His sometimes well-founded, sometimes speculative books are a continuing source of inspiration for later media theorists, including the author of this book. Any book that bases itself on or reacts against McLuhan's work can be considered to belong to the school of pure media theory. The second, non-literary source for media theory is information and communication theory, which was developed by the cyberneticists of the 1940s, whose most important representatives in this context were Claude Shannon (1916–2001) and Gregory Bateson (1904–1980). Finally, a third pillar of classical media theory is the philosophy of symbolic forms, articulated in the 1920s by Ernst Cassirer[2] (1874–1945) and further developed in the 1950s by Susanne K. Langer (1895–1985).

In *Understanding Media Theory* these three schools are used to elucidate each other. The original literature is referred to in the notes but is not dealt with explicitly. I retain concepts and approaches from classical media theory books which have proved durable in the course of fifteen years of teaching film and television students, activists, future artists and designers-in-training. Works in the Bibliography were selected chiefly for readability. References to useful but less gripping reading matter can be found in the books mentioned in the Bibliography.

Media theory is aimed at understanding media, but it also considers itself a product of media. This double consciousness is characteristic of every interaction with media. Media show us the world, but at the same time they so change us that we believe the world they show us is the only real one. Put another way, media so change us that we believe our medium to be the ideal means of perceiving, representing and calling forth the world. Or changing the world so that it becomes real. Media do not so much show us how life really is; rather, they give us the feeling that we can only experience real life by connecting to them. Or else they cause an aversive reaction, and make us feel that life is only real once we get outside their reach, deep in the wild or on the last pristine beach. Both reactions, for and against, are evoked by the media themselves, and not by any deep internal core of authenticity. What is authentic about people is how they deal with media. We cannot escape the media, but we can certainly understand them.

# Media Theory: The New Science

Media theory informs us that we take our communications media so for granted that we fail to see all the tricks they're pulling on us. One could say the same about life, of course. We are so embedded in life on Earth that we do not see the ways in which we are limited or shaped by it. It would take the perspective of an extraterrestrial intelligence to identify the sort of things we worry about and to know whether they are appropriate, sensible, worthwhile, absurd or dangerous. Science tries to assume such an external point of view while remaining on Earth, to see how everything is going on the planet, how it's changing and can be changed. This is true of the natural sciences as well as the social sciences.

Media theory tries to assume such an alien point of view in studying the means whereby we communicate with each other, and with which media theory itself is brought into being. Marshall McLuhan dubbed media theory "the new science," although we could probably better call it a science in its infancy. But then again, all the sciences, including physics and biology, are still just beginning to get insight into and deal responsibly with earthly and cosmic phenomena (the universe, for example, at present consists of 70 percent dark matter or dark energy – in other words, stuff we don't yet have any means of observing or understanding). So we can safely call media theory a science. But we must establish what the capabilities and limitations of its scientific potential are.

## The Origin of Media

Every science must begin with the birth of its subject.[1] The first question we must therefore ask is: Where do media come from? or, What was the first medium? There has been a good deal of speculation about this. It could have been dance; that is, movements of the body that are consciously performed so that they evoke an added meaning. In dance, this meaning is the influence of invisible forces at work between people's bodies, and between people and things in their environment – forces that dance makes visible by representing or evoking them. Animals dance too: bees indicate where certain foods can be found by dancing in front of their hives. Other candidates for the role of earliest medium are sign language (such as that used by apes); the babbling with which all children begin to speak; the human urge for decoration, in which, slowly but surely, something more than decoration becomes visible (an animal or person, for example); our natural inclination to fantasize away until patterns appear in our wild imaginings, and then become myths, and thus explanations of the world – but to tell myths, we need speech. A question that precedes the media question seems to be: Is the body itself a medium, a means of transmitting a message in coded form from a sender to a receiver and vice versa? This question is not an easy one to answer.

All we can perceive of the world around us is the way our bodies react to it. Feelings and emotions are the sources of all knowledge. What the world is or does independently of us humans is beyond our grasp, just as it is for animals and plants. Machines can observe independently of humans — think of measuring instruments and security cameras — but we never perceive more of these machines than the way our body reacts to them. We do not know what it is we are perceiving, but we know how our body processes those perceptions into images, into representations of something we experience as outside and separate from ourselves.[2] In this sense, the body does seem to be a true medium: the only thing media show us plainly is how they process input into output. This output – the message that reaches the receiver – says at least as much about the medium the message was sent through as it does about the sender that has sent the input through the medium.

The body is the origin of all media, but it is not a medium itself – except when it is consciously used as one, such as by the Bushmen (see box opposite page). Media are products of the body which have become independent of it. Think of a drawing on a rock face or a sheet of paper: you recognize the human hand in them, but the hand itself is gone. Or the telephone: the handset with a whole telephone network behind it is a medium, but the telephone conversation isn't; it falls under the "body" heading. A pair of binoculars is a medium; the bird observed through it is not (the message of the bird is its visible silhouette). Thus the webcam is a medium, but the bedroom secrets that are made public through it are not. A distinction can be made between medium and message, although it must be acknowledged that no message sent through a medium – and that includes the seagull flying overhead – exists independently of that medium. Without binoculars the gull would have remained an unrecognizable dot. Against a blue sky all birds are black – that is, until you point your binoculars at them.

## The Body as a Medium: Bushman Presentiments

The Bushmen feel in their bodies that certain events are going to happen. There is a kind of beating of the flesh, which tells them things. Those who are stupid, do not understand these teachings; they disobey them, and get into trouble – such as being killed by a lion, etc. The beating tell those who understand them, which way they are not to go, and which arrow they had better not use, and also warn them, when many people are coming to the house on a wagon. They inform people where they can find the person of whom they are in search, *i.e.* which way they must go to seek him succesfully. The Bushman, when an ostrich is coming and is scratching the back of its neck with its foot, feels the tapping in the lower part of the back of his own neck; at the same place where the ostrich is scratching. The springbok, when coming, scratches itself with its horns, and with its foot; then the Bushman feels the tapping. When a woman who had gone away is returning to the house, the man who is sitting there, feels on his shoulder the thong with which the woman's child is slung over her shoulders; he feels the sensation there.

_Xáken-an explains: "The Bushmen's letters* are in their bodies. They (the letters) speak, they move, they make their (the Bushmen's) bodies move. They (the Bushmen) order the others to be silent; a man is altogether still, when he feels that his body is tapping (inside). With regard to an old wound, a Bushman feels a tapping at the wound's place, while the tapping feels that the man (who has the old wound) walks, moving his body. The one man feels the other moving his body; he says to the children: 'Look ye around for grandfather, for grandfather seems to be coming; this is why I feel the place of his body's old wound.' The children look around; the children perceive the man coming. They say to their father: 'A man is coming yonder.' Their father says to them: 'Grandfather (his own father) comes yonder; he would come to me; he was the one whose coming I felt at the place of his old wound. I wanted you to see that he is really coming. For ye contradict my presentiment, which speaks truly.'"

*The word *!gwe* was used by the Bushmen to denote both letters and books. ||*kábbo* explained that the beating in their bodies, here described, are the Bushman's 'letters', and resemble the letters which take a message or an account of what happens in another place.

From: W.H.I. Bleek and L.C. Lloyd, *Specimens of Bushman Folklore*, London 1911.

## The Definition of Media

"Media are means of reaching others; that is the simplest definition."[3] It is also the most general. This universal conception of media defines the calls and songs of birds as media, and the roaring of animals, and even the pheromones female moths secrete to lure males and the ones beetles use to lead each other to sources of food. According to this definition, even the pollen of flowering plants is a medium, because it is a means by which flowers bridge the distance between them. Here we are speaking of the extreme end of media theory, which describes the entire living world as one big information-processing system whose various parts continuously communicate to each other the states they are in and their responses to previously received messages. The universe itself is understood as a collection of media, for planets, stars and galaxies communicate with each other by means of gravity, light and other kinds of radiation. Speculative writings have even been published which consider reality as a digital computer.[4]

"Media are extensions of our senses into the public domain." This is the specific definition of media.[5] Every medium amplifies the function of a particular sense – the lens and the webcam extend the range of action of the eye. At the same time, that medium numbs or "amputates" the remaining senses, such as smell and touch. It's not just that we seldom smell what we see with the help of media. The reason the sound in the cinema is turned up so high is because we wouldn't hear the soundtrack otherwise, so concentrated are we on the overwhelming visual imagery our eyes must process. Media are extensions of elements of the body, of the organs devoted to perceiving, monitoring and regulating that body. The senses are the organs that call forth emotions in the body.

Alongside the externally oriented senses – sight, hearing, smell, taste, touch and sense of balance – we possess many senses inside our bodies. These register the states of various chemical and physical equilibria, such as levels of hormones, acidity and sugar levels. The internal senses make homeostasis possible in the internal environment; that is, the dynamic, physical and chemical balance that must be maintained to keep our cells and molecules active. If we include these internal senses in our definition of media, then narcotics and stimulants are also media, and so are medicines. If one continues down this road, one could see perfumes as media of smell, and salt and other flavor enhancers media of taste.

A somewhat different definition of media is used in this book: a medium is a technological or artificial extension of a bodily faculty. This concept of medium encompasses more than just the senses. Walking is not a sense, but a bicycle is a medium of transport, a technological device which extends the body's capacity for locomotion by means of wheels and handlebars. The message sent with a bicycle is the cyclist's body. Since energy and matter are two manifestations of the same phenomenon, in this definition of media it makes no difference whether one is transmitting information on a wire or electromagnetic waves or sending things via a transport medium. Electric light is a medium, because it extends vision in time: it lets us see something for longer in what would otherwise have been the dark (for longer than a candle, and with a greater range). The same is true of glasses where age is concerned: glasses lengthen the active life of an intellectual (reading, writing, observing, teaching) by decades.

Spoken language is a phenomenon at the boundary of nature and technology. It is part of the body as well as an extension of that body into the public domain. Our power of speech enables us to reach others and be reached by others without leaving our bodies. The same goes for sign language and other forms of nonverbal communication. Unamplified – without loudspeaker or signal flags – these are not media, but bodily abilities. Media are means of amplifying input from the world within our bodies, but also, inversely, of expanding our bodies' potential for action in the world. With media, traffic is always two-way. This is true of all technology. On the one hand, technology allows us to get to know the world better or differently than we could without its support; on the other, it provides us with a means of intervening in that world. The simplest way of getting to know the world is always to reach out, change it, and see what happens.

## The Birth of Media Theory

Marshall McLuhan called media theory a science because, like all sciences, it can explain all of reality – but only from a single angle or on a single level. Physics can interpret essentially every phenomenon in the universe as obeying natural laws. Biology considers everything from a microbe to an ecosphere as a living and evolving system. Chemistry sees bonds between atoms and molecules forming and breaking everywhere. In the same way, everything can be interpreted culturally, or sociologically, or historically. Media theory understands every phenomenon and process as determined by the media with which it is brought into being, interprets itself, is perceived and stored, and finally made into something else.

This concentration on one aspect of reality allows media theory, like physics and biology, to perceive phenomena that would remain invisible without its particular perspective. Like other sciences, media theory consists of statements about empirical phenomena. It always explains these phenomena, however, as media interactions, whether they are cultural, social, biological, physical or chemical processes or some other kind. Like other sciences, media theory makes all-encompassing claims; I will say more about this in a moment.

The central proposition by which media theory attempts to explain everything is "The medium is the message." This is a tautology, a statement along the lines of A = A. And this is its power. Every science consists of descriptions of phenomena which are connected to each other with the help of a tautology so that an explanation of the described phenomena flows out. "To map the description onto tautology," Gregory Bateson called it.[6] Biology derives its coherence from evolutionary theory, whose central idea is the survival of the fittest. This, too, is a tautological statement: in evolution, species survive because they are the "fittest," and we know they are the "fittest" because they have survived. We can explain the whole organic world by asking about every characteristic of an organism, "What makes this advantageous for survival?" or "Why does this makes this species or population of plants or animals 'fit' or 'fitter'?" In a similar way, we can explain the whole technological world using media theory by relating descriptions of it to the statement "The medium is the message."

Marshall McLuhan wrote, "The printing press is more important than any book ever printed" – that is, it has a greater social, cultural, psychological and political impact. "The medium is the message" means the knowledge that a medium transmits is greater than the knowledge that people transmit using it. The experiences a medium brings about affect us more deeply than the experiences we bring about using it. The medium does something more, or something different, than what we intend to use it for. We do not change each other through the information we transmit to each other using media, but through the fact that both of us are hooking up to a medium and letting ourselves be influenced by it in a like or analogous manner. Connecting to another consists of finding a common medium.

Media theory tries to see a part of reality that remains invisible from any other scientific approach. That is, it endeavors to see how we look at the world. It tries to hear how we listen, to say how we speak, and so on. Media theory seeks an expansion of consciousness. For a large part of our active existence we are connected to media. They are at least as familiar to us as our pets and others who are close to us. Only when we use new or unfamiliar media do we need to think about them, and then we think mainly about how they work and not about what they are doing to us. We accept their existence, however critical we probably are about their content. We experience little without media.

Historically speaking, awareness of the medial nature of all human expression and perception was late in coming, somewhere around the beginning of the twentieth century. Cubism in painting – such as early Picasso and Braque – was the first artistic movement to confront viewers with the fact that when they looked at a painting, they were seeing a painted piece of canvas, a construction dreamt up and executed by a painter. Regarded as a medium, a painting is no more than that: paint on canvas, set down as fields, lines and points. Before cubism, paintings were intended to create the illusion of representing something other than themselves, a space containing a person or a landscape, or else a representation of the painter's unique vision of these phenomena outside the painting.

But the cubists said: No, a painting is not a natural representation of something else, something spatial with a third dimension reaching deep into the canvas. The painting is two-dimensional: its inside and outside, front and back, top and bottom and all the rest lie on a flat plane. The point is not to look at the canvas bit by bit; you must take in the whole thing at one glance. Then you will see, as if for the first time, that you are looking at a medium instead of a message, instead of a so-called representation of something in the "real" world. That real world is an illusion in painting; only the painting itself is real, as a medium. This view of cubism led Marshall McLuhan to say, "The medium is the message."[7] And this statement proved applicable to all media.

Marshall McLuhan got the essence of his media theory from the cubists, who were the first representatives of what became known as Modernism in art. Modernism is the will to be modern – that is, the will to connect to the latest media. If one wants to be modern, and preferably as modern as possible, one can do nothing else but allow one's worldview to be determined by the newest medium and the newest technology, for only media and technologies change and can therefore be modern: the world itself remains as old as ever. Biologically speaking, for the past hundred thousand years humanity has stayed the same, but using technological means, we have made the environment in which we live more and more intelligent, in the sense of containing ever-greater amounts of information, knowledge and potential for action.

According to McLuhan, the cubists linked their painting to the medium of film, which was still new at the beginning of the twentieth century. All modernist twentieth-century art – poetry, literature, sculpture, music, ballet, film, photography, video art, and so on – links the medium through which it manifests itself to a more modern medium, in the hope of discovering what is unique and irreplaceable about its own, older medium. Modernist art legitimizes itself not through building on an illustrious past, but through the special, authentic characteristics of the medium in which it is created. Modernist art is art that seeks to engage the medium itself – written language, clay, bronze, notes, movements, poses, pictures. Modernist artists try to get the medium to propagate a message no person ever would have hit on – an extra-human message, because it is purely medial. Modernist art is art that seeks to make its medium its message.

"The medium is the message" is thus a tautology as well as a historical observation and an artistic project. The fact that the modernist project was conceived and executed in the twentieth century demands an explanation. Such an explanation would immediately answer the question of why no one had realized before that a painting was nothing more than paint on canvas, plus the illusions the combination creates for the viewer. The question of what makes media so invisible, or rather so transparent that we do not notice them while we are using them to look at our surroundings, will be discussed in the chapter "General Media Theory." The chapter "Historical Media Theory" will describe how the introduction of a new medium – such as alphabetic writing in ancient Greece – leads to a realization of the mediality of the previous medium (poetry, in Greece), and even to a strict renunciation of the older medium in favor of the self-knowledge that the new medium makes possible.

The accelerated introduction of ever-newer media in the twentieth century was what made possible the high media consciousness of the people of the twentieth century. Artists were always the first to figure out that their own media were only media and not means of ultimate revelation. Time after time, there appeared avant-gardes that recognized their own media as mere technological means and treated them accordingly. Poetry became a monument to language in language, painting a monument to painting in painting; sculpture was no longer about anything but sculpture. Art became medium-specific, and its practitioners therefore called their work "autonomous," or even "absolute."

In the modernist experience of life, media are about media, not about anything outside themselves. This "outside" is an effect of media, an illusion conjured up by media to legitimize themselves. This legitimation is necessary, for who would use media if they told us nothing more than how they themselves work, told us nothing about the outside world? The answer is that contact with media in itself brings forth strange, moving, pleasant and horrible experiences in the bodies of the users, with or without reference to something outside. It is no accident that media use as well as drug use soared to historic proportions worldwide in the twentieth century. "General Media Theory" will also discuss various aspects of this.

## The Limitations of Media Theory

Put a camera in a meeting hall and everyone will start to behave differently. Point a camera at a baby and she will smile. Observing reality with the help of media influences that reality in a way comparable to the way quantum-mechanical phenomena arise because there is a physicist observing them. The world does not come into being because we are observing it, in a cause-and-effect way, but it does take on the manifestation in which we observe it as soon as we do so. In other words, reality does not exist independently of the media with which it is registered. And it never did – even when people had little more than myths, cave paintings, drawings on animal skins, and hills and valleys as points of reference in the landscapes they inhabited. Nor did it when René Descartes and Isaac Newton[8] established that space and time exist independently and are thus in that sense absolute. According to these founders of modern physics, our observations can approach this absoluteness (with the right measuring equipment), but it can only be purely expressed through mathematical formulas and geometric figures. According to media theory, too, space and time are relative because they are dependent on our observations, and those observations are determined by the media through which they are made. In observing and describing the world, it is not the world that is the message, but the medium – even if that medium is mathematics. Media theory is a post-Newtonian science.

Modernism called itself modern because it opposed tradition. But that tradition was, and is, borne by media just as much as is the modern attitude to life. Even in the New Testament, human history was described as characterized by a medium from the first moment: "In the beginning was the Word." It is no coincidence that this discovery was made in a written text. The biblical text continues: "And the Word was with God, and the Word was God." So God is a medium, He is a word: language. The evangelist goes on to say that the word was made flesh in the person of Jesus. Something similar is true for all media: they begin as a potential in our bodies, expand into the public domain, creating a world – and finally end again in the body, as a way of being, a range of feeling, a worldview, a belief system.

We are our media. And because we are never the only ones using a medium, as media users we are always part of a crowd. With some media, this crowd appears literally, such as with lectures, concerts, theatrical performances or film. With others, it remains imaginary: we must imagine it as we use the medium. With television, the crowd appears in the form of ratings; with radio, in the form of listeners who phone in; with youth TV stations, as e-mailing or texting viewers; with newspapers, as circulation figures; on websites, in the page hit count. We read books alone, but it makes us part of a language community. In the media we are never alone. Media are ideal antidotes to loneliness.

Modernism tried to divest itself of the illusions that sprang from the traditional representational use of media – media do not represent, they present, as it was said; they do not imitate, they create. At the same time, modernism gave rise to its own illusion when it claimed that media could only speak about themselves (and that what they had to say was brilliant, moving, profound, tragic, real). The modernist illusion called upon a scientific worldview in which reality consisted only of matter and energy. Anything else we believed we saw sprang from the imagination. This conception of scientific knowledge was Newtonian and, in that sense, antiquated, though the modernists embraced it blindly: the world consists not only of matter and energy but also of information. Information refers to the form in which matter and energy manifest themselves. A picture is an accumulation of matter or light in which something else can be discerned besides that matter or light, namely the thing that the image is depicting, referring to. This something else is information. Information is everything in an image that one knows could have looked some other way.

If nothing else can be seen in an accumulation of matter and light, then it is not an image, whatever else it might be. The modernists' answer to this criticism could have been that the "something else" – the information – distinguishable in their autonomous, non-referential images consists of the fact that they are paintings (or sculptures). This means that the information content of modernist art is extremely low: the only information it contains is that it is art. For the early cubists this was no problem, because, surprisingly enough, in their autonomous work there is plenty to see that does not belong to the painting itself: a portrait of an art dealer, for example, or a French landscape or a Spanish village. Only the abstract painters, and especially the action painters after them, succeeded in making paintings that sought only to be paintings and nothing more.

But every human creation refers to something else. Even music refers to more than the sounds that make it up; perhaps we should say that there is more at play in music than the instruments it is made with. If there were not, it would touch no one. Music has a much more direct connection to the body than any image – it follows the rules and dialogues of feeling rather than those of reason, and it tells us more about the rhythmic and melodic passage of time than about the extent of space.[9] Thus, words are groups of sounds or letters that refer to something other than the sounds and letters themselves – they refer to life, in us and outside us. This reference to life is not so much the meaning of the words as the reason we are willing to use them in the first place – willing to speak, or to read what another has written.

In every medium, there is something that touches the outside, the extramedial – that which the medium is about and yet is outside the medium's reach, though it can be evoked, suggested, extolled. The extramedial, by definition, cannot be represented with media; if it could, it would be intramedial. Yet the extramedial can only be experienced thanks to media; we feel its presence before we have understood anything of the meaning of a work. Some poems have it, as do some photographs, some music, some installations. Other art does not. Or might suddenly if one returns to it later. But only when the extramedial is there can we summon up the energy to study a photograph, savor and ponder a poem, give a piece of music our attention instead of letting it wash over us, or take up the challenge of engaging with an interactive installation.

Only after one has noticed the extramedial does one ask questions like: "Why is this word here and not another?" or "Why do those trees and bushes hang under the line of the horizon like that in this photograph?" or "Why that hiccup in the melody, or that slightly too-short beat after that held note?" With skillfully made poetry, photography or music, we feel admiration for the creator's or performer's craft, but with "really good" work, we begin to feel grateful for the existence of life itself. The meaning of sentences, images and sounds is secondary; the extramedial charge is always experienced first and transcends the experience of what we have seen or read, until ... well, until what exactly? The extramedial is not matter, energy or information. It is a fourth element that is called forth by means of mediation. Our sense of this extramedial is something to be refined our whole lives long, until we die.

Science seeks to describe and explain all of reality. Modernism sought to shape and transform all of reality. We have seen that media theory seeks to interpret and fathom all of reality. Now, we will go a step further. We will leave Modernism behind – including the postmodern variety – and embrace a broader notion of science than the materialistic one of its founders, and of the researchers of the neo-materialistic worldview. Media theory cannot describe all of reality. Media-theoretical description finds its limits in the certainty that there is a domain outside the media which remains inaccessible to media and media theory. Acknowledging the extramedial will prevent media theory from developing the totalitarian tendency to try to explain everything, and thus to control and change it. Only our existence in the media can be controlled and changed; nothing else can. The media have their limits. Past those limits, even media theory can do nothing.

# General Media Theory

## Introduction

"The medium is the message." This sentence is the core of media theory, but at the same time it is a joke, a distortion of the central thesis of information theory, which holds that communication occurs when a sender sends a message through a channel to a receiver, who then either responds or does not (see box on page 29).

Information theory and media theory both try to answer the question of what exactly is being transmitted or exchanged when we communicate and use media. According to information theory, this is a certain precisely quantifiable amount of data, diluted with a certain equally quantifiable amount of noise. Information is measurable regardless of the medium in which it is sent. According to media theory, there is much more going on in communication than just an exchange of information: the medium influences the sender as well as the receiver. Information theory pays no attention to how it does this. Every medium influences both poles of communication in its own characteristic way.

In the first place, the medium determines what information can and cannot be transmitted. In fact, most information sent through a medium says more about the characteristics of the medium itself than about anything else. McLuhan expressed this aspect of communication in the aphorism "The medium is the message." In the second place, the medium evokes in the sender as well as in the receiver a certain more or less definable environment – a mental space or sphere of interest in which users of the medium can understand each other because they share a way of seeing, pre-formed by the medium, while those unconnected to it have no clue what's being talked about. McLuhan summed up this aspect in another aphorism: "The medium is the massage." Every medium massages its users into a crowd, a more or less unified group of users. Because information theory is the perverted, often unacknowledged foundation of media theory, we will first address the concept of "information" and later the more medial notion of "environment." As these two ideas are joined together through the concept of "feeling," general media theory will emerge.

# Communication

# The Concept of "Information"

Information is not the same thing as meaning. A statement's meaning says nothing about its information content. An utterly profound statement can contain the same amount of information as total nonsense. Within every medial expression or communicative act, three levels can be distinguished: one to do with information, one with meaning, and the last with the effects of one or the other.[1] The first level is technical in nature. It concerns the precision with which the symbols of communication are transmitted from sender to receiver. The sender is the source of information. The message this sender transmits can consist of anything: a series of letters, electrical pulses, electromagnetic waves, brushstrokes on a canvas, sculpted clay, cast bronze, or pixels glowing on a monitor. The kind of carrier has no influence on the message's information content. Technically speaking, it is of no importance whether the message is about anything or means anything. All that falls within the technical domain is the question of whether and how the information sent from the source (book, telephone, radio station, painter, sculptor, video artist, net artist, computer) gets to the receiver. How many pulses were sent by the sender and how many have gotten to the receiver? And have any been added, lost or garbled (noise) along the way? The second level is semantic in nature. It concerns the question of how the symbols that are sent precisely transmit the desired meaning. You cannot interpret information; you can only send it. That information's meaning, conversely, can be interpreted. The meaning is the element that determines how long the information transfer will continue: when both parties have the impression that the message has come through, or at least become understandable, they will end the exchange. The semantic level of communication is highly dependent on the first, technical level: if the information hasn't come through, there won't be any meaning. On the other hand, a perfect information transfer says nothing about the comprehensibility of the message. The third level is social in nature. It concerns the effectiveness with which the sent meaning influences the receiver's behavior in the way desired by the sender. In military communication, what matters is whether the order that has been given is actually followed. The subordinate must not only indicate he or she has understood the order ("Copy that"), but also report when it has been carried out and with what consequence. This is called "command and control." In artistic communication, what matters is whether a poem or video installation has been understood as its makers intended (the semantic level), but also whether the viewers have been aesthetically affected, and how deep this runs or how much reflection it provokes. With music and theater this third level expresses itself in the audience's response, which in turn raises the performance levels of the musicians or actors on stage. With more stable art forms, an artist never knows for sure whether his or her work is having the intended effect, because there is a time lag between the production and the reception of a work. This offers the consolation that if no effect can be detected, there might yet be one for a future generation. On the other hand, with much art, what the desired effect might be is a mystery. Also, the effect of art is often so subtle that it is practically impossible for audience members to tell that they have changed in some way. But only if they have changed is art present: the difficulty of saying anything about the effectiveness of art as communication does not mean that this third level is not important. It is crucial.

Information is a measure of the freedom of choice one has when selecting a certain message. Mathematically speaking, the smallest possible choice is between 0 and 1. It was Claude E. Shannon who, building on the work of a few predecessors, took this smallest choice as a unit of information and named it the "binary digit," or "bit" for short. If you type the word "the," your freedom of choice with respect to the next word is already limited: a noun must almost certainly come next. An adjective might precede it. The chance that an article, adverb, preposition or verb will follow "the" is very small. Thus the freedom of choice – or the information – of the statement drops as soon as you say "the." The more arbitrary a statement, the greater its information content: if you're spouting nonsense, any existent or nonexistent word can follow "the." Ravings almost always contain more information than meaningful statements do. The more improbable a statement, the more informative it is. When one cannot predict what the next word will be, every word acquires a maximum charge: much contemporary poetry is based on this principle. The drawback of using this as a strategy is that the higher a message's information content is, the smaller is the chance that its meaning will come through or it will have much effect.

When you code information into a particular signal and send it via a medium to a receiver who decodes it back into the original message, if noise has been added to the signal during transfer, its informa-

## The Communication Model of Information Theory

The communication system may be symbolically represented as follows:

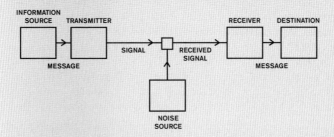

The *information source* selects a desired *message* out of a set of possible messages. The selected message may consist of written or spoken words, or of pictures, music etc.

The *transmitter* changes this *message* into the *signal* which is actually sent over the *communication channel* from the transmitter to the *receiver*. In the case of telephony, the channel is a wire, the signal a varying electrical current on this wire; the transmitter is the set of devices (telephone transmitter, etc.) which change the sound pressure of the voice into the varying electrical current. In telegraphy, the transmitter codes written words into sequences of interrupted currents of varying lengths (dots, dashes, spaces). In oral speech, the information source is the brain, the transmitter is the voice mechanism producing the varying sound pressure (the signal), which is transmitted through the air (the channel). In radio, the channel is simply space (or the aether, if any one still prefers that antiquated and misleading word), and the signal is the electromagnetic wave which is transmitted.

The *receiver* is a sort of inverse transmitter, changing the transmitted signal back into a message, and handing this message on to the destination. When I talk to you, my brain is the information source, yours the destination; my vocal system is the transmitter, and your ear and the associated eighth nerve is the receiver.

In the process of being transmitted, it is unfortunately characteristic that certain things are added to the signal which were not intended by the information source. These unwanted additions may be distortions of sound (in telephony, for example) or static (in radio), or distortions in shape or shading of picture (television), or errors in transmission (telegraphy or facsimile), etc. All these changes in the transmitted signal are called *noise*.

From: Claude E. Shannon and Warren Weaver, *The Mathematical Theory of Communication*, Urbana 1949.

tion content will rise and the message's improbability, its complexity, will increase. Noise is any information in a message that was not intended by the sender. In English approximately 50 percent of written language is redundant; that is, if you leave out most vowels and a number of consonants, you can still tell what it says. (In some written languages, such as Hebrew, vowels are always left out.) Still, it is wise to include all the letters in a message, because the redundant information can neutralize the influence of noise. The "extra" letters make it easier to tell what was intended and what was distorted in transfer; for instance, spelling mistakes are easy to spot. Redundancy enables the receiver to bring the information content of a noisy message back onto the semantic level at which the message's meaning can be guessed. In other words, it is inadvisable to work in the most stripped-down, compact possible way if one has clear intentions and wants to convey them to readers, viewers or listeners. On the other hand, too many familiar, likely words in a sentence make a statement low in information and therefore uninteresting.

The concept of "information" can also be used in situations where it is not a human who is choosing from among a collection of possible messages, but nature – for example, with respect to the shape of a leaf on a plant or a limb on an animal. A smooth-edged leaf contains less information than one with an irregular edge. This is because you can hardly predict from one point on an irregular leaf where the next one will be; this isn't a problem with a smooth edge. An irregular edge is less likely than a smooth one, and therefore more informative.

Asymmetrical organisms thus contain more information than symmetrically built ones. More complex forms, phenomena and situations are always more informative than their simpler counterparts. For this reason, we can say that nature consists not only of matter and energy but also of information.[2] As Gregory Bateson put it, "Information is any difference that makes a difference."[3] Whether a leaf is slightly discolored does not matter if what you want to know is which tree it came from. What is informative is whether the leaf's edge is thickened, rolled, wavy, perfect, indented, serrated, toothed, lobed or split. The choices on which a phenomenon's information is based can also be made by a machine such as a computer. The beauty of the bit is that the 0/1 combination can be translated into on/off (e.g., for switches) or open/closed (for gates). So a mathematical operation can be converted into a technologically realizable machine, for instance a digital computer with all its programmability. For this reason, information theory forms the theoretical basis of the information society, or age, we are said to be living in.

Our age and society are characterized by the continuous production, dissemination and processing of information; meaning plays a secondary role. Machines are very good at making choices and thereby generating information – a computer can design a building or draw up a school roster. But it is thus far nearly impossible for a machine to create meaning, or even to grasp it. The semantic level of communication is difficult to computerize, as is evidenced in the slow development of computer image recognition, among other things. Machines can communicate brilliantly in the sense of exchanging information, but they seldom have a good conversation.

The concept of "information" makes clear that nature and technology can get along fine without meaning, but we and other intelligent beings can do so much less easily. We are more inclined to seek an explanation or judgment of a phenomenon than to try to observe it as closely as possible. Meaning not only offers us something to hold onto in a complex world, it allows us to forget all phenomena before our very eyes whose meaning we know. This allows us to drive or bicycle through the city without being overwhelmed by the information bombarding us: we need pay no attention to things we recognize. We can easily navigate the remaining amount of information.

The meaning level of communication serves as a kind of screen between us and the world – a screen through which we see certain things but no longer see others, for as long as communication lasts. One of the objectives of modern art was to break through this screen of meaning, so that things would reappear before our astonished eyes, totally meaningless in all their autonomy, as a mass of matter, energy and – we can now add – amoral information. For anything that is pure information, devoid of meaning, lies beyond good and evil.

Modern art sought to wipe the gaze clean and cleanse language of its cliches and stereotypes, so that stones became stones, animals became animals, and birds became birds, and no longer symbolized anything other than themselves (chilliness or durability, innocence or savagery, freedom or wanderlust). Modern art sought to let things stand for themselves alone instead of imposing our will and subjectivity upon them – in other words, contaminating them with human meaning. Purity, purity! Modern art did not seek to use media to transmit something other than themselves; it wanted to let them purely express themselves. They wanted to allow them to be themselves in the hope that – what? That a secret would be revealed? I will say more about this later (in the section "Touch and suspicion" on page 65).

Information is not matter or energy. Since the more unlikely a phenomenon or artifact (a statement, an image, an object) is, the more informative it is, we can say that information is the relationship between the known and the unknown. A relationship is not a thing, although you can give it a name; it is something between things, something you observe or construct by means of perception and interpretation. When you gather information by looking at something, particles or waves do not enter your body from the world through your retinas to be translated into a representation or perception in the visual cortex. Nor does the reverse happen when you disseminate information.

To describe information as a relationship between known and unknown is to ignore its bodily aspect and make an intellectual or psychological phenomenon of it. Yet information is definitely a bodily process too. Bodies, like all living systems, are "autopoetic."[4] That is, every element of the body, from cells and tissues to organs and larger systems, is constantly busy falling apart and dying, but it is also constantly busy restoring itself, replacing and expanding. This permanent reconstruction process not only makes the body resistant to the second law of thermodynamics ("spontaneous processes always tend toward entropy"), it also makes it flexible, capable of withstanding and overcoming all possible injuries and disturbances.

One such disturbance is the series of events known as "information processing." When the eye perceives something, the biological balance in the rods and cones of the retina is disturbed by the incoming light. The individual sensory cells in the eye get rid of the disturbance – and thus restore their equilibrium – by issuing a chemical signal to the neurons of the optic nerve behind them. To compensate for this disturbance of its own equilibrium, the optic nerve in turn transmits an electrical impulse to the neurons behind it, and finally to the brain, where the neurons compensate for disturbance by distributing the impulse over various areas of the brain. These, in turn, deal with disturbance by stimulating certain organs and muscles to act via neural pathways, thus finally extinguishing the original disturbance.

We experience this process as perception, as action, as statement – as "information processing," the basis for all intelligent behavior. Series of small, all-or-nothing steps take place in the body in which neurons either are or are not stimulated. The passing on of stimulation is not coordinated at any central point. Neurologically speaking, there is no central control mechanism, no nerve core where all the pathways come together or branch out from, where the soul or the self is located. There are only clusters of neural pathways and brain areas which are activated over and over, starting an interaction for every perception, every sensation, every memory. An external observer, however, will see the process very differently: he or she will see an individual reacting to a stimulus either appropriately or pointlessly, or more precisely, he or she will describe that reaction as a form of intelligent (or foolish) behavior. Every person is an observer and describer of what happens in his or her own body. From the shore, a submarine navigating between rocky islands appears to be purposefully avoiding the cliffs and staying in deep water, but inside the craft, the crew is merely making sure the depth gauges on the control panels stay in their prescribed positions as much as possible – so many meters above the ocean floor, so many meters from the coast, and so on. In biological systems, these prescribed positions are fixed in an internal environment kept more or less constant through the process of homeostasis. That is, throughout the body, internal senses monitor whether hormone levels, temperature, pH, sugar content and so forth are staying within the accepted margins – if not, the body reacts to correct the too-high or too-low values.

This continual repair in the context of homeostasis creates a continually unstable balance, a dynamic equilibrium maintained more or less all one's life, and this forms the background against which all the shorter repair cycles of sensory disturbances and memory outpourings in the brain take place. Out of this combination of short and long repair cycles comes consciousness, the feeling that you are continuously there and that you are the being that knows this. You recognize others' bodily reactions to external and internal disturbances as emotions. You experience your own reactions as feelings, if you experience them at all. And one of those feelings is you.[5]

The methods for keeping biological gauges in their prescribed positions – the routes along which abnormalities in the body's state of equilibrium are remedied – arise in the course of earlier reactions, through trial and error. Some reactions, some neural and hormonal discharge routes, are found to thoroughly put an end to the disturbance; others cause a new disturbance (if you react clumsily, you bump your head; if your body temperature goes up too high, you become very ill). The more external stimuli you process, the better you train your system to effectively handle disturbances to its internal equilibrium. In human evolution the capacity for language has proved to be a remarkably effective means of neutralizing sources of disturbance – but also of deliberately putting them into action.

In sum, information is neither a substance nor a relationship, but a bodily process. Language does not have an autonomous meaning, it has a communicative function. Knowledge is a pattern of neural routes in the body which is created, repairs and transforms through the knowledge process itself. Communication is not a transfer of information but a link between two or more biological systems which continually disturb and repair each other. What a system itself thinks it is doing and what an external observer thinks it is doing give rise to two descriptions that have little in common with each other. One uses a different conceptual apparatus inside a system than one does outside it. Inside the system, there is knowledge: yes or no, on or off, millions of times over. Outside the system, there is intelligence, uncertainty, emotion, consciousness, love.

## The Concept of "Environment"

Very young children who do not yet know the meanings of words are nonetheless very capable of understanding when their parents talk to them. This is possible thanks to the mother's or father's vocal intonation. In almost all cultures, parents transmit four basic signals to their children through tone of voice: encouragement, disapproval, attention and comfort. These four intonations can be not only electronically imitated but also electronically detected. A robot can be built that can hear the emotional charge of what is said to it. It can then reply in a matching tone, though only in babble. (Getting a robot to speak completely automatically in sensible language for very long is still impossible.) When one of these robots communicates with a person, the person is able to understand what it means. Most adults react somewhat awkwardly, but children quickly enter into whole conversations with the robot.[6]

In "friendly" communication, the information content of what is said is apparently not very important. As long as we have the feeling of being understood, the conversation can continue. The robot, too, understands the emotional charge of what is said to it, since it responds adequately. We have just seen that in an information exchange, the decisive factor in how long a conversation will last is meaning. As long as the people have the impression of not understanding each other, the two-way information stream will continue. If, however, the conversation is mainly social in nature, the information exchange will go on as long as they have the impression they are being understood: in this case, meaning is what keeps the information streams going.

At the end of such a conversation – with a robot if necessary – both partners can come away with the impression of having had a pleasant or even useful talk. This is because one of the ways in which people grasp or invent the meaning of a certain quantity of information is to order the information as they talk. A pattern, and meaning, thus follow naturally. Explaining to someone else what you are doing is an effective way of understanding it yourself.

People understand each other when they think the same way, and they think the same way when they use the same media. Objectively observing the world, objectively describing it, objectively providing this description to others, and finally drawing a conclusion from this logically ordered information – one that is not only universally valid but can also be translated into rational behavior – all these acts are so unnatural that it takes years of scientific education and practice to start getting the hang of it. If one does at all.

The idea that objective observation, description, reporting and thinking are possible, even if it is contrary to common sense, is a consequence of the medium of writing. By writing down words and arranging them in lines, you achieve such a distance from what you are asserting that you are able to see where your emotions, feelings, intuitions, instincts, tastes, conscience and memory, and your social position, role and status, distort, color or otherwise subjectively influence your observations and comments. This distance through writing makes the scientific method possible, but the knowledge that is derived in this way is itself in turn distorted, colored and limited by the characteristics of the medium of writing. The users of a medium are inevitably programmed by it (to use a computing metaphor). A new medium teaches us to see, hear, smell, feel and taste things that were previously outside our reach. This is profit. But there is also a loss: everything we came to know through other media, or without media, is forgotten on the spot. This is why when a new medium is introduced in a society, there are invariably cries that now civilization will truly perish from superficiality, stupidity or forgetfulness. What is meant by "civilization" is written culture – but remember what destruction that culture itself caused when it eliminated the oral one, with its sacred attitude to life, its gods, demons, rituals, myths and hero songs.

The point of communication is not to transfer information, to foster understanding, to convince or to be convinced. This is merely the "content" of the communication or of the media (I will say more about this in the next chapter). The effects of the use of a means of communication are much more far-reaching than information theory makes clear with its model of sender-medium-receiver. What is essential in communication is not what the sender intends, for the sender's message is almost wholly determined by the medium in which he or she makes that intention public. Imagine that a message or intention could exist independently of the medium with which it was disseminated: then it would not matter whether one expressed something in the form of a poem, a painting, an opera, a film, a TV show, a novel, a phone conversation, a photograph, a ballet, a theatrical performance, a scribble in a margin, a website, a city park, a lecture ... Even when the message is something general, like "peace," or "anger," or "time and space," the properties of the medium will have a deeper effect on the audience than the underlying concepts. Nor can one search for the most suitable medium for each message, because what one's message is is determined by one's medium – one must therefore first find the medium that best suits oneself, and after that, with a little effort, the message will come of its own accord.

To understand media, we must pay attention not to what they are meant to do, but to their effects. Every medium has things it takes for granted, a normality and an observation pattern all its own; McLuhan called all this its "environment" (see box on page 38). This environment encompasses everything on which a given medium exerts influence, from social and political institutions and the way public life is organized to the citizens' mentality and sense of decency, and even the feeling about what gives life meaning, or what is the highest achievable truth, beauty or good. In an "environment," not only is the corresponding medium seen as normal, everything that can get through its filter is normal and understandable. Anything that cannot be grasped through the medium, however, remains strange and incomprehensible.

The effect of the transport medium of the car is not that you can use it to get from A to B (this is its content). Its effect is that the whole landscape and all of public space is reorganized around it – road networks, gas stations, garages, parking lots, shopping centers, motels, suburbs, high-rise apartment blocks and office parks, all of which generate experiences and lives of their own. The car is an extension of our ability to move, and it gives the driver the sense of his or her body being literally extended to the bumpers. The speed of the car causes all distances to shrink, but this gain in time causes the traversed landscape to lose its inherent value: it has no meaning anymore when one is racing through it along an eight-lane highway. And all previous forms of movement, such as riding on horseback or in carriages, pass at once into the realm of folklore or other forms of recreation, and are no longer functional.

The effect of the telephone, and of all electronic media, is not that it lets us hold a conversation over long distances but that it connects us directly with every other person/user on earth. Everyone is reachable by phone, including every artist and scientist in the world. Why not call up your heroes? The effect of photography is not what you see in your vacation snapshots, but the certainty that only the present truly exists, for only the present can be photographically recorded. The rest of time, the past and the future, exist only in the imagination. Old pictures show an old present. We live in a "permanent now," a "continuous present" – this was the dominant attitude in the twentieth century.

You can define normality as the part of reality you do not need to consciously perceive, because it will function regardless. Information was defined above as an unlikely combination of elements. Normality, therefore, consists of everything that is probable and thus does not inform. Because of its ultra-low information content, those who are part of normality perceive that normality with extreme difficulty. Normality consists of all the things that simply are because they are, and every rule of behavior that we follow because that's the way it's done. Media theory tries to show that normality is not a natural,

## Marshall McLuhan on Environment and Art

"The medium is the message" means, in terms of the electronic age, that a totally new environment has been created. The "content" of this new environment is the old mechanized environment of the industrial age. The new environment reprocesses the old one as radically as TV is reprocessing the film. For the "content" of TV is the movie. TV is environmental and imperceptible, like all environments. We are aware only of the "content" or the old environment. When machine production was new, it gradually created an environment whose content was the old environment of agrarian life and the arts and crafts. This older environment was elevated to an art form by the new mechanical environment. The machine turned Nature into an art form. For the first time men began to regard Nature as a source of aesthetic and spiritual values. They began to marvel that earlier ages had been so unaware of the world of Nature as art. Each new technology creates an environment that is itself regarded as corrupt and degrading. Yet the new one turns its predecessor into an art form. When writing was new, Plato transformed the old oral dialogue into an art form. When printing was new the Middle Ages became an art form. "The Elizabethan world view" was a view of the Middle Ages. And the industrial age turned the Renaissance into an art form as seen in the work of Jacob Burckhardt. Siegfried Giedion, in turn, has in the electric age taught us how to see the entire process of mechanization as an art process *(Mechanization Takes Command)*.

As our proliferating technologies have created a whole series of new environments, men have become aware of the arts as "anti-environments" or "counter-environments" that provide us with the means of perceiving the environment itself. For, as Edward T. Hall has explained in *The Silent Language*, men are never aware of the ground rules of their environmental systems or cultures. Today technologies and their consequent environments succeed each other so rapidly that one environment makes us aware of the next. Technologies begin to perform the function of art in making us aware of the psychic and social consequences of technology.

Art as anti-environment becomes more than ever a means of training perception and judgment. Art offered as a consumer commodity rather than as a means of training perception is as ludicrous and snobbish as ever. Media study at once opens the doors of perception. And here it is that the young can do top-level research work. The teacher has only to invite the student to do as complete an inventory as possible. Any child can list the effects of the telephone or the radio or the motor car in shaping the life and work of his friends and his society. An inclusive list of media effects opens many unexpected avenues of awareness and investigation.

From: Marshall McLuhan, *Understanding Media*, New York 1964.

inevitable environment, however much people take it for granted, but a consequence of the communication technologies that evoke it without anyone noticing.

Art is a method of creating distance from the normality evoked by a medium without making the audience leave that normality behind. Art can create an "anti-environment" in which everything that was probable before suddenly begins to show unlikely features and thus penetrates consciousness – without, however, ending in terror. For the opposite of normality is terror. From the outset, terror's aim is to block every normality. Power means forcing others to worry about the wrong questions – questions that should have been answered within normality. If any aspect of daily existence can contain vital information, if nothing is probable and everything that looks probable must be deeply distrusted because a secret agenda could be lurking behind it, such terror leads to a crippling of the ability to act. Fear rules. Art is anti-normality, but it is also anti-terror.

Art is not self-expression; if it were, it would only show the limitations the medium imposes on the artist. No artistic form is necessary for expressing yourself: frowning, whining, laughing, running around and slapping yourself on the forehead are clear enough. Rather, art is the expression of a medium. Normality must be disrupted now and then if it is to remain normal instead of hardening into conformity taken too far. This disruption is art. Art shows reality as disrupted normality. Or one might say it shows a reality by disrupting normality. It is able to do this because it not only represents or evokes but lets us see this representation and evocation. It shows the message as well as the medium. It shows that escaping the media is not only impossible, but also undesirable.

Without media, we can experience nothing, know nothing, be nothing. But out of this nothing – the extramedial – comes art. Art keeps the channel to the non-medial open. Art shows the extramedial *in* media. The extramedial can only be experienced through media, not as something that is missing, but as the absurd, the intangible, the unpredictable – that fragile something without which art would have no point, would be nothing but bold attempts to impress. A prelinguistic level of experience, one of powerlessness and surrender. Once the extramedial touches us in a medium, art is present. Art initiates us into the media via the extramedial. Art initiates us into the culture via an extracultural experience.

Because media are always mass media, and in a given cultural phase one or more media always determine what we see, each of the various phases can be characterized in terms of the dominant medium, or the dominant environment or normality. Thus we can distinguish between an oral culture, a written one, a "typographic" or print one, an electronic one, a visual or image one, and a digital one. Finer distinctions can also be made. Let us take the field of visual culture. The term "visual culture" signifies the realization that the printed word's leading role in the recording and dissemination of information has been taken over by the technical image – in the shaping of public opinion, the tourism industry, political processes, medical procedures, military strategies or anything else. The world is understood more and more in images and less and less in words. In the field of art, the term "visual culture" signifies the realization that drawing or painting or sculpture is just one among many kinds of images artists can work with, not the only one, or even the most important, suited to be a carrier of art. In visual culture, art can be made not only with traditional media but also with technical media. Images (pictures, depictions, representations) can be distinguished in terms of the manner in which they were brought into being. The photograph was the first technical image in the world, the first to be made with a machine. Prephotographic images are handmade, traditionally produced. Photographic images are photomechanical records of existing situations. Postphotographic images are the optical results of computer calculations. Prephotographic images are cave paintings, drawings, paintings, etchings and lithographs, but also statues. A photographic image is any technical image with a chemical or electromagnetic carrier (such as analog photography, film and video). A postphotographic image is any technical image set down on an electronic carrier in the form of digital code – any artificial, synthetic image. Once a photograph made with light has been scanned and digitized, it is postphotographic. This convenient division can be used to explain every existing way of understanding images. If someone contends that images come from a deep human need for preservation and permanence, it is evidence of their preference for prephotographic images. Traditional images' material carriers make them so durable that they last, as it were, for eternity. This claim is also made about the meanings of traditional images: these are believed to be as durable as their carriers ("eternal values").

This notion seems strange to those who are moved by photographic images. The photographic is devoted to immediacy, the preservation of an instant, the permanent now. Photographs have no duration; they are made in a fraction of a second. They are splinters of time, traces of space. All that really exists in photographic consciousness is the fragment of the present – no continuity, no movement through time. Finally, postphotographic images are not even immediate: they are merely fleeting. They are, as Vilém Flusser put it, not two-dimensional but non-dimensional.[7] If one changes a number here and there in a postphotographic image's numerical code, one will see something very different on the screen. Stable postphotographic images are no more than silences or breaks in an endless, unlimited image metamorphosis. For postphotographic consciousness, all that exist are continuity, flow and flux; there is no standing still anymore.

More is at stake here than just interpretations of the nature of images. Deliberate types, those made happy by contemplation, obviously have a consciousness formed by traditional images, for these are images whose significance or meaning we are meant to deduce through careful consideration. Traditional images are part of a tradition, a narrative, and we can learn to read these in images if we pay the necessary attention. Those who find it much more important to observe what is actually there to be seen than to sit around contemplating things are lovers of the photographic image. This kind of image simply registers what is recordable and doesn't worry about meaning at all. But those who find pure observation much too passive and would rather actively intervene in the existing state of affairs – their hearts belong to the postphotographic image, with all its internal possibilities for manipulation. These three patterns of thinking can be found everywhere things are made visible.

Let us take architecture as an example. The carrier of this medium is material, physical in nature – stone, wood, textile, concrete, steel, glass – and thus we can regard architecture as a traditional medium, comparable to sculpture. This explains the trouble, and the fascination, architects have with the technical imagery of photography, film, video and virtual reality. Seen from within the scope of architecture, these media are fundamentally incomprehensible. This is clearly evident in the work of Paul Virilio. In book after book, Virilio raises a protest against the power of the technical image. He has linked far-reaching conclusions to the immediacy and fleetingness of these images with respect to the decay of cities and the demise of democracy.[8] Seen from the perspective of his own media – city planning and architecture – his argument is perfectly true, for the time frame of traditional media is eternity. Seen from the point of view of the technical media, however, Virilio's concerns are neither here nor there. Of course images are transitory; of course buildings are torn down after a while. No human effort is meant to last forever. Everything ages. Everything – including the technical media themselves – perishes in the end. To a consciousness founded on the immediacy and fleetingness of the technical image, the decay of cities is nothing to worry about. On the contrary: for technical consciousness, this decay constitutes the foundation of city planning.

## Hot and Cold Media

Information transfer may not be the most important part of communication, but the amount and level of detail of the data transferred does determine how effectively it can generate an environment and what the nature of that environment will be. A drawing of a cow need consist of little more than an outline of the animal, plus a bit of shading to symbolize the spots on the coat, and probably a straight line to indicate the horizon, or bumpy lines to suggest trees in the background. These few lines are enough for the viewer to place the cow in context. The pink nose, the heavy body, the green grass, the blue sky, the shady foliage: one imagines it without effort, and not even explicitly. Suggestion is enough for us to understand the whole picture, or at least what it is supposed to "be."

When we see a photograph of a cow in a pasture with trees, on the other hand, every millimeter is filled with photographic grains or pixels. Nothing is left to the visual imagination: the picture is complete, full, saturated. Photography is said to be a "warm" medium because the sense it addresses itself to – the eye – is overfed with information and thereby "heated." Drawing, by contrast, is a "cool" medium, for the eye receives little information and is thus not heated – but the imagination is. A hot medium heats up the corresponding sense while leaving the imagination cold. A cool medium does little to the corresponding sense, but heats up the imagination.

Photography is a cooler medium than film. With a photograph, we can or must imagine what happened before and after the moment of recording; in a film we can see it. On the other hand, film is cooler than webcams and security cameras, because the viewer must imagine the parts that have been edited out of the cinematic narrative, while on a security video or a website we can see everything, at least as far as the camera allows. The essence of the distinction between cool and hot media is the extent of involvement generated in the media users or the audience. The less information there is, the more involvement there is. The less we know, the more we make up. The more we make up, the more interested we are. And the more interested we are, the more inclined we are to believe.

The reason some telephone conversations are so much more spontaneous and pleasant than meetings in person is because the telephone is a cold medium compared with conversing in the flesh. Because of the lack of visual information received on the phone, we get a completely different picture of the person on the other end of the line than when we can see his or her physical reactions. We could say that we develop an image of the other that is auditory in nature rather than visual. And this can have favorable results for both parties.

The abovementioned law – the less information, the more involvement – has important cultural and artistic consequences. There are three possible reactions a work of art can seek to provoke in its audience. First of all, it can arouse desire – a will to possess what is represented or to buy the work itself, or else a feeling of lack because we have neither and never will. Second, a work of art can seduce us. The viewer or listener does not know what is happening to him or her, but feels that what is represented is in some way personally addressed to him or her and demands a response. Third, art can fascinate us. Fascination means feeling irresistibly moved to look at or touch something or someone, but no urge whatsoever to act. Paralyzed, we watch without ever averting our gaze. Our critical faculties are switched off, but not our desire to look. Generating information overload is a good way to arouse fascination.

Hot media evoke desires (porn is a hot medium). Cold media seduce (by activating the imagination). Overheated media fascinate (by killing off will and imagination). Hot media work with meaning: the viewer sees what is shown and what kind of response it calls for. Cold media work "semiurgically": that is to say, what is represented could have or acquire meaning, but is as yet an enigma. A response is called for – but which one? If one accepts the seduction, a game begins, the compulsory rules of which only gradually become clear.

Overheated media are completely meaningless; this is their power. They work according to a secret rule: "The senseless is irresistible in every sense."[9] One can imagine that cool media could also generate fascination: so little information is provided, or such vague information, that there is no meaning to discover in it. This probably explains the spread of hand-painted Japanese characters in Western culture, like the circle drawn with one stroke that stands for who knows what. There is always something fascinating about the exotic, for the exotic is anything whose meaning is unknown (as soon as someone translates that Japanese circle symbol, it will no longer be exotic but banal).

The preceding makes clear that the notions of "hot" and "cold" media coined by McLuhan can be used in various ways. We can differentiate between media according to temperature – photography is a hot medium, caricature a cool one. But a medium can also be made hot, or used in a cool way. Hot and cold – like the statements about the medium being the message and the massage – are not just descriptive terms, they are also strategic ones. Some photographers are able to capture light in such a way that the result is cool and stimulates the power of imagination, and thus seduces. This can be done by means of the amount of light or shadow, gray tones, or the obscureness of the situation depicted, or in some other way.

Photographers can also bring a visual bombardment together in a single image so that the result fascinates – as, for instance, photographs of corpses sometimes do, or the curves of a body. With this kind of fascinating photography, what counts is not so much the fullness of the image (the fact that so much is going on in it) as the intensity of the depiction. A photograph can make a body so photogenic that the viewer is dumbstruck. Glamour photographs fascinate, but arouse no desire (in any case, no erotic desire). A male or female body in a photograph can either titillate and arouse desire, or seduce us and make us envision a whole new relationship with ourselves and our fellow humans, or fascinate us and leave us empty-handed, at once stunned and exalted.

In practice it is extraordinarily difficult to know whether an artist or art movement has chosen a medium because it is cool or hot, or made cool or hot whatever medium happens to be available. Consider the church. Catholicism is a religion of the image, and Protestantism is a religion of the word. The first uses decoration, ornamentation, embroidered robes, processions, devotional pictures, Madonna figures and numerous rituals. The second uses monotony, tedium, long sermons and prayers, slow hymns and attention to the Word. Islam is also hostile to the image and glorifies the word.

The Reformation, in which the Protestant church split from the Catholic church, consisted in the first place of a "breaking of the images" and a whitewashing: every image of Jesus, Mary and the saints was smashed or covered in white paint and the flags that had hung in churches were burned. It was no coincidence that the Reformation took place shortly after the invention of printing. For more than a thousand years, the Bible had been read solely by priests, in Latin. In the fifteenth century it was suddenly mass-printed in the national languages and distributed. The images that until then had propagated the Christian message promptly lost their meaning and became symbols of the power of the church and its falsification of God's word.

The Reformation came down to a potent reduction of information. In the Protestant church, the only information a believer gets is what the minister disseminates: there is nothing (attractive) to see. But the less information is disseminated, the greater the degree to which the imaginative power of those who receive it fills in what is missing. The Catholic church was and is a hot medium, in its buildings as well as its liturgy and daily religious practice. Here, the rule is: long for salvation, but do not imagine anything more than that. The confessional, too, is a hot medium: keep nothing secret, tell it all, bring all your little sins to light, those natural desires that sometimes drive you to commit wrongful acts. Confession frees you of them and makes your desire pure once more.

The Calvinist and Lutheran church are cold media: no pictures, no chatter. Religious life takes place entirely within the believer, inside the world of his or her imagination. The Catholic church does not demand that its believers maintain any personal relationship with God, as long as they go to church and do their religious duty. The Protestant church insists on a personal bond with the Creator. The believers can bring this about only by fully using their power of imagination; otherwise His hand will not be discernable in all manner of apparently insignificant events. In a similar way, television can be used in hot, cold and overheated ways. McLuhan's view was that watching television made the younger generation more intelligent; he himself understood nothing of what he saw. Few media are as capable of provoking fascination as easily as television. Even the most idiotic game show is sufficient to cripple the viewer's will to such a degree that he can no longer rouse himself to turn off the set or change the channel. Neurological research has found that areas of the brain associated with critical thinking show scarcely any activity during television viewing, but are immediately reactivated as soon as the set is switched off. This explains why it is so difficult to turn off the TV – when you're being lazy, not thinking is more pleasant than thinking. This finding seems to suggest that the medium of television is inherently overheated, and thus crippling to the will. Yet this is not true, for there are always TV producers who refuse to accept that their medium is "stupid." They use their "zero medium"[10] artistically, in an attempt to make viewers intelligent, conscious, critical – and they often succeed.

The theory that television is inherently hot is no more true from a historical perspective. TV was introduced in the culture around 1950 and spread like wildfire – first in bars and other public spaces, then in the living room, and finally in every other room of the house, right down to the bathroom. The picture on first-generation sets was vague, blurry and streaky – screens were small, picture lines were few, programming was dull. Meanwhile, film had become more beautiful than ever, with pricey spectacles projected on giant screens in Technicolor. And yet the mass audience preferred to watch TV. Feature films were a hot medium; television was cool. Film had suddenly become mere entertainment, while television provoked deep involvement. Because of this involvement, the first generation of American children to grow up with television, when it went to university in the 1960s, became the "protest generation," which felt personally responsible for all the suffering in the world.

The United States lost the Vietnam War because of the introduction of color television, which showed the American public in a luridly realistic manner what "our boys" were doing and experiencing over there. Conversely, color television became a commercial success because it portrayed the war so grippingly. Yet the audience's involvement in what it saw diminished rapidly – color TV is hotter than black and white. It was not a coincidence that the offspring of the protest generation became the first consumer generation: they wanted everything they saw on TV, and in other hot media, like magazines, movies and ads. All over the world, children exposed to hot media still want a better life – not only richer in terms of the primary necessities, but also richer in experience. The power of imagination is one of the most important social factors with which we can change our given reality. Images of a fuller life already exist – all we have to do is make them reality in our own lives. And if the imagination sees no way out under the given circumstances, if the ruling regime and the inherited economic situation have little more to offer than boredom and mindless work, one can always try to emigrate to the place where the pretty pictures come from: "Moving images meet mobile audiences."[11] By the 1930s large groups of American retirees were leaving the Midwest for Hollywood in the hope of getting a piece of the good life.[12]

Information reduction is the key to all great cultural upheavals. It was the one great strategy all the twentieth-century artistic avant-gardes had in common. Abstract art contains much less information than realistic or representational art because it contains no references to an outside world. Malevich's painting of a black square contained, in principle, one bit of information – until the paint began to show craquelure and its information content noticeably increased. Pop art, in turn, contained less information than abstract art, because there was no underlying idea any more, as Andy Warhol emphasized.[13] Minimalist art contained even less information than pop art, simply because there was much less to see. And conceptual art contained less information than minimalism, because there was no longer even a work of art any more, only an idea, a "concept." The fact that so many contemporary artists make works out of garbage is likewise part of this strategy: practically all information has been drained from the material by the time it is joyfully rediscovered in a trash can or garbage dump.

It is undoubtedly true that in the twentieth century the number of images on earth increased enormously, as did the number of people. At the same time, it is clear that the new media of telephone, radio and other unstable carriers such as television, internet and mobile telephone have had a far more radical influence on the twentieth-century sense of space and time than any of the more traditional media, like photography (instant painting), film (moving photography) and video (transformative film). The more numerous and hotter pictures got, the less important they became. People knelt before carvings of the Madonna and child; they are less inclined to do so before a Madonna music video. In our time, the important images are medical photographs, of one's own baby, tumor or brain activity: all cool images. Also important are the weather photographs that determine how one's plane will fly. The information contained in these pictures is a matter of life and death. Other images are little more than entertainment, aimed at achieving medial effects – they do not incite us to make decisions. And the same is true of any image intended or used in an artistic way.

The distinction between hot and cold media says nothing about the kind of information that is created or transmitted in a given medium; it indicates only how much of that information there is, how precise it is, and in particular what its effects on the receiver will be. It describes two ways in which media play on the receiver's senses. Perception is not passive registration of the outside world on a neurological carrier, with subjective noise added. The image of the outside world is actively constructed, not only by the senses and the brain but by the entire body.[14]
Space is not something that already exists, through which we can move without thought. Space is brought about in the brain through movement. Our feet and knees help us to build space just as our eyes and ears do. Babies and toddlers do little more than practice perception by crawling and running about, bumping into things, grabbing things, and falling down. We can see them literally building their world with their bodies. Or: we can see them literally building their bodies with their world. Only when one has mastered the perception process does it become possible to perceive without moving, so that one can lie on the sofa and watch TV or consume a movie in a theater.
Because perception is learned in the years from which no conscious memories are preserved (up to the age of four), it remains a largely preconscious process all our lives. One continuously augments one's picture of the world, and only extremely rarely is one beset by doubts about the validity of that picture. If you only see the front of a table, how do you know it has a back? You don't; you imagine one. Imagination is necessary for perception. More than that, if you do not use your fantasy, you will notice awfully little of the existence of the world. Night after night, we train our imaginations by dreaming. People who are slowly going blind continue to see their telephones, coffee cups and pen trays sitting where they always have for some time – until the fateful moment when the coffee cup is set down somewhere else and they reach out and grasp thin air, however clearly they think they saw the cup.

Media are technical means of increasing the reach of the senses. They are extensions of the body in space and time. This is why media have profound effects upon the process of perception, or the way we construct the world through registration and imagination. A hot medium stimulates one sense so strongly that the heat can only be subdued by allowing all the other senses to cool, that is, making them numb. A cold medium does the opposite: it deadens one sense so severely that the remaining senses are activated and produce emotion. In the cinema the body is "switched off," so to speak, by means of darkness and a comfortable seat – only the eyes and ears can perceive. These senses are subsequently bombarded with information. With the projected images and sounds, for the duration of the movie, an attempt is made to stimulate the bodies of the audience – with eroticism, suspense, sympathy, fear. Watching a film in a theater is as total and totalitarian an experience as driving a car, and it happens equally without thought. Drivers are, in effect, watching a film being shown on the windshield of the car. Hot media are narcotic; they cause anesthesia. They shut us off from the world. And that can be wonderful.

Cold media are stimulants. A cold medium stimulates all the senses, even those it is not directed at. This is why a piece of music, a statue, a photograph or even a minimalist film can create the impression of spreading through the whole world and being about everything. Some music makes us think, "That was beautifully played." But the occasional song, tune, symphony or concert makes us think, "Life is beautiful." Or "What a mystery existence is." We can think this because all our senses are activated and open, but focused on something other than the impressions we are consciously taking in. This inherent vagueness is salutary, universal, divine – in any case, the opposite of totalitarian. It makes us better than we were. It gives us confidence in ourselves and the world.

This cannot be said of hot media, which cause a combination of exaltation and pain, and then just leave you there. The credits roll and the party's over. But with cold media, that's when it really starts. Hot media fragment the body's experience; cold media integrate it. Each strategy has its pleasant and less pleasant sides. "Hot" and "cold" are not moral judgments or standards of quality. They are descriptive terms: they describe medial strategies.

Remediation

# The Content of Media

If you see a tree or a flower, or someone walking by on the street, or you look at the clouds or a parked car or the television or your mother, what exactly are you looking at? Common sense has it that one is looking at objects and people as they exist in the world. Something similar is true for statements such as "Look at the cloud." The ultimate meaning of the word "cloud" is the cloud itself. If someone asks "How are you doing?" the content of the question is the other person's physical and mental welfare. But this is not the way it is. Nothing is just an object, and no one is just a person. Every object is a perceived object, every person the perception of a person.

What we perceive is not the thing so much as the emotional response that that thing evokes in us. More than that, we do not perceive things but the relationships between them, the connections and interactions between them, and between them and us. The objective world is for us doubled by a world of experience. Seeing an object is never a neutral process, because it always activates certain experiences and pushes out others. We do not have complete control over our experiences. They organize themselves into certain relationships and into a certain system – a worldview – which, however, is not a "view" in the sense of a two- or three-dimensional representation but a landscape of intensities of feeling, preferences and aversions through which we navigate as we perceive and react, literally "by feel."

Perceiving objects, shapes standing out against a background, is something we must learn to do. Take birds as an example. If you set off into open country armed with binoculars and a bird-watching guide in the hope of discovering what kinds of species live there, you will be sorely disappointed. Just as to a city child every small bird is a sparrow, except some sparrows are yellower or redder than others, for the beginning birder every bird is more or less brown with lighter spots here and there. On your own you will see nothing to speak of. Only when one has been on a few excursions with experienced birdwatchers does one begin to recognize shapes, stripes on wings and tails, spots on a breast, the color of a beak or a leg, and so on. What is at first little more than a speck in a tree becomes a source of information – not only of the name of its species but also of its age, sex, population, behavior and more. You can even recognize a bird by its call and its song, by how it sits on a branch, by its silhouette, and by where it is found.

Experience is not just the shock we get when we see something unlikely and thereby receive a dose of information to process. Experience is also the ability, built up over the course of many "shocks," to translate certain intensities of feeling into words – for instance, the name of a bird one has seen – or into behaviors, varying from running away to taking action. A woodworker senses what he can do with his wood, a writer in the process of writing feels where her text is going, a programmer feels the direction in which a solution must be sought. Every perception, every expression and every behavior is founded on experience. By the time you become conscious of what you are doing, you already have years of experience with your own behavior; from birth one has done little else besides amass knowledge about it. "An experience" is another term for a shock, "experience" a synonym for an experience over the long term.

The content of the perception of a tree is not the tree itself, but the experience with trees one has had over the years – call it one's knowledge of trees. If you ask someone how they are doing, you call up a whole world of affects, aversions, affinities, fears and desires. Media play a leading role in all these experiences, simply because we know the world largely through the media, and know the media largely because we put our experiences into them. That we think we see depth in a flat painting is not an absurd illusion, as many modernist painters claimed. We really do see depth, because the painting stirs the experience of depth which we carry around with us. Yet we do not confuse the painted space with the space outside, because we construct our experience of the actual space not only with our sight but also with our sense of touch, with movements and resistances, with faraway and nearby sounds, with fading or echoing voices. Painted space is purely visual – not illusory so much as virtual, a virtual space: visible, but not tangible. We also see this kind of space in mirrors and photographs.

Pictures evoke virtual space, stories evoke virtual history – a closed and independent system which, if all is well, links to the system of self-organized experiences which we carry within us and which, to a considerable degree, we *are* (more about this in part 3, *The Virtual Object of Interactive Art*). It is not true that "unmediated" experiences are more real than experiences created by media: they are the same, but stimulated by different sources. We do not have two separate experience systems in our brains and our bodies, one of which is activated only by media and the other only by direct perception. Medial experiences are as spontaneous as unmediated ones; the accompanying feelings are just as authentic. You could accuse nature of aiming for a cheap effect with a splendidly radiant sunset. You could also wonder how that effect was achieved, not in the atmosphere but in yourself: what in you is responding, and how? What matters is not the realness of the sunset, but you: how precisely tuned is your feeling?

The virtual, visual space of a painting – to develop this example – is constructed by the painter with colors, lines and fields suggesting shapes. The experiences we have with space generally consist of what we see, hear and feel in it, and what we remember and imagine in connection with it. These kinds of experiences must be evoked on the canvas solely through visual, artistic means. For this reason, painters depict objects in a way that suggests interaction between them; out of this interaction spring visible space and the palpable continuity of that space. This interaction consists of variations in color, the directions of lines and their positions relative to each other, brush technique, rendering of texture, and so on. The canvas comes to life for the viewer because his or her eyes are focusing on its various elements in turn.[15]

In short, space in a painting is not represented but created. A color field with a line is enough to evoke a meadow with a tree. Even Malevich's dark square creates a feeling of space. Painting is the use of color to create a three-dimensional space on a flat surface. This virtual space organizes itself between the shapes on that surface. The shapes can refer to objects from the existing world, but that is not how they derive their effect. The painted tree, cow, city, water, people and clouds derive their emotional value in no way from what they represent or depict, but solely from the space they generate – at least where art is concerned. Kitsch works in the opposite way: the tearful gypsy child is what moves us, not the way in which it was rendered in space (or evokes a space around it).

Henri Matisse: "Expression, to my way of thinking, does not consist of the passion mirrored upon a human face or betrayed by a violent gesture. The whole arrangement of my picture is expressive. The place occupied by the figures or objects, the empty spaces around them, the proportions – everything plays a part ... A work of art must carry in itself its complete significance and impose it upon the beholder even before he can identify the subject matter. When I see the Giotto frescoes in Padua I do not trouble to recognize which scene of the life of

Christ I have before me, but I perceive instantly the sentiment which radiates from it and which is instinct in the composition in every line and color. The title will only serve to confirm my impression."

A painting is not about the reality that is depicted in it, but the way in which it conjures up a reality by artistic means, thus creating a real feeling of space in the viewer. The virtual space on the canvas assumes the form of an existing space for the viewer. The medium of painting is the only message, but we, the viewers, are its content. The reason a painting does not derive its meaning from an "outside" but carries all its meaning within itself, as Matisse said, is because the virtual space of painting is not a continuation of the space the viewer is in, but is separated from it by means of a frame, a white wall, the edge of the canvas, or something else. The virtual space in a mirror looks like an extension of the existing space. A mirror is not "expressive" but reproductive. Also, in a mirror we are not inclined to consider one part of the picture more successful or more stirring than another: a reflection is neutral. A painting, by contrast, is the expression of a feeling, an experience – that is, a thought that cannot be expressed in words, but only in this particular painting.

Exactly the same thing that happens in paintings also happens in photographs, although it took many generations for painters and art lovers to accept this. The classic objection to photography was that a painted virtual space was much more visual than a photographed one, simply because traces of brushes and other painters' tools are left behind in paint, so that the painted image retains a certain tactility. A painting is not only the expression of a feeling in a virtual space, but also an expression of a body in existing matter. As a consequence of this, a viewer always sees a painted image as a construction – a constructed picture. By contrast, a photograph appears to be a direct translation of light falling on objects into a two-dimensional picture. It was said that a photograph was nothing more than a copy of space, or a sample of it. It was therefore incapable of generating the exalted emotions that painting had held a patent on from time immemorial.

Photographs, however, are just as constructed and as capable of arousing feelings of exaltation or humility as paintings are. Photography is not about an outside world which happens to exist and is registered by photographic means – "objectively," since, at least in the photochemical material that makes up the image, no trace of a body can be detected. Assisted by the appearances of objects, a photograph evokes the same kind of virtual space as a painting: a space independent of the one the viewer is in, a space which carries its meaning in itself and in a comparable way links itself to the self-organized experiences of the viewer. Any decent photograph has a foreground, a middle ground and a background, and lines and fields suggesting depth. Lesser photographers point their lenses at objects; better ones aim at the space between them. Even portrait photography can be spatial, whether that space is around the person or in his or her face or body.

Of course, a photographer can deliberately filter all depth out of his or her image. The effect of this can be very powerful for an audience expecting to see depth there. In painting, too, there are painters who want nothing to do with spatial illusions, but instead seek to confront the audience with the truth of the totally flat surface. These experiments, too, are only unlikely and informative if one expects to see a virtual space when turning one's gaze toward a painting. The reason many modernist painters deliberately started to paint flat was because photography had shown that painting was not the only medium that could create virtual space by means of color – photography could even do it with grays alone. The reason postmodernist photographers deliberately photographed flat was because they took the criticism of their modernist colleagues to heart.

A photograph is not about the outside world, but about the manner in which it is able, using photographic means, to evoke the experience of a space in which objects are arranged. Those objects are arranged in that way because the photographer arranged them in that way in the viewfinder while circling around them and gazing through the lens. A photographer can photograph a space in such a way that it looks static, so that the viewer experiences timelessness. In this stilled photography, time seems translated into space: one moment has been taken out of the course of history and made absolute. But a photographer can also photograph a space so that instead of hanging between objects like an immovable gap, that space forms a dynamic link connecting all the bodies and objects in the picture together – and also connecting them to the viewer's gaze. This kind of images "really move us": we feel a desire to put a hand on that crocheted bathing suit, join in that family party. If a photograph does something to us, the effect is always a medial one – even when you are moved at seeing a photograph of your child, what moves you is not the child but the photograph: it is what is able to mobilize your feelings for your loved one.

"The content of a medium is always a previous medium." This statement by Marshall McLuhan means that we only understand a new medium because we see the ways in which it imitates an old medium. The reason people in the 1830s understood what they were seeing on daguerreotypes' strange shining plates was because they knew that lines, fields and spots could depict something other than themselves, namely people, landscapes or buildings. They knew this because they were familiar with painting. Painting is the content of photography. A photograph generates the same kind of virtual space as a painting because photography reproduces painting's linear perspective – the main way of representing virtual space in Western art since the Renaissance. To think that what for centuries had been considered the unique ability of painting was in fact only a technical trick, a mechanical, computerizable process!

Photography, in turn, is the content of film. This is literally true: a reel of film is a series of photographs stuck together. When a film is run through a projector, the photographs appear to move on the screen. Film adds movement and sound to the experience of virtual space, which makes it a more effective medium than photography and also a more convenient one – easier to consume (although movement in film is also virtual, because it does not stimulate the proprioceptic organs with which our bodies perceive movement). Film is related to photography as prose is to poetry. Film, in turn, is the content of video: video consists of film images whose color, composition and structure can be manipulated using various techniques. Film and video are likewise the content of television. And television is the content of webcams. Film is also the content of virtual reality – three-dimensional, this time, but with the central perspective, movement and sound preserved. Or to give an example of a different sequence: spoken language is the content of written text, and written text is the content of printed text.

As the quotation in the box on page 38 shows, Marshall McLuhan applied his own rule extremely liberally. The content of the environment created by a medium is the environment of a previous medium. The content of the electronic age is the mechanical age. This is to say that we generally worry about problems associated with older media, while uncritically accepting the medium that makes us who we are. "Who we are" is made up of the feelings evoked, magnified and intensified by the new medium. The problems of older media consist of feelings we no longer take for granted and therefore have come to see as important, difficult, significant or beautiful. The feelings evoked by normality come to be seen as less valuable and less real than the old. The experiences we undergo through new media are still so fresh that they are inaccessible to reflection, unless works of art are made out of them (at least, according to McLuhan).

McLuhan said many times that we were like drivers speeding toward the future while looking in the rearview mirror. What he meant was that our society is constantly introducing new technologies and media and allowing them to turn our whole lives upside down while continuing to worry about problems associated with older media. McLuhan was articulating a typical twentieth-century avant-garde idea: ordinary people do not realize what is happening to them; only artists understand something about their own era, and even about the future. The reason artists of the previous generation are honored while contemporary ones are not is that most people need about 25 years to develop a consciousness as relevant to the present time as that which is available to avant-garde artists right now. This is why art from a gen- eration ago is valued as "real art" while contemporary work is deemed rubbish, as in "my kid could do better than that."

According to McLuhan, avant-garde art formed an "anti- environment," a kind of antidote to the environment being propagated through society by the latest dominant medium. Modern art was an "early warning system" that showed what kind of social and psycho- logical blows would be dealt by new media and new technologies. To fulfill this momentous task, artists had to hook themselves up to the newest media and let the effects of those media play out in their work and in themselves. This was precisely what artistic modernism was: the will to be modern was the will to blindly throw oneself into the latest medium and then, slowly but surely, learn to look. Poets wrote poetry as if it were a series of simultaneous radio programs; architects de- signed buildings as if they were fighter jets; painters studied television to understand how to make the shallowest possible images ... Avant- garde art is art that ignores its relationship with the audience in order to enter fully into in the workings of its medium.

But is this idea correct – is the content of every medium a previous medium? Do we always worry about older media and outdated experi- ences while taking no notice of the newest medium and our true feelings? Is painting photography's sole content, and photography film's sole content? No. The history of nineteenth- and twentieth-century painting shows that it wasn't just the new photographers who were imitating the old painters by making picturesque images. After 1839, the painters also tried to imitate photography – in fact to resist it – initially by making painting as realistic as photography was considered to be: as precise, as perspectival, as banal and exalted, but in color instead of photographic black and white. The results were attractive but pointless, and after the first wave of pictorial realism, painters went in search of techniques possible in painting alone, because these would legitimize painting's independent existence alongside photography.

What photography was considered incapable of doing because of its mechanical objectivity was reproducing a subjective experience of reality. Impressionism based itself on this personal approach. An image of reality could only be "real" if the eye, brain and hand of the visual artist had touched it. Later, cubist painting used the singular technique of representing people, things and landscapes from multiple perspectives at once, in contrast to photography's single camera angle. Expressionism, and surrealism after it, declared the inner (dream) world the only true reality and sought to depict it. Thus the links between painting and visible reality were becoming looser and looser. Once painting from live models had gone out of fashion, painting was able to develop into pure abstraction, into minimalist painting. Abstract paintings are concerned with the question of what about them is real: not the interpretation of a canvas as a window on a depicted space, nor the experience of the viewer, but the material and the geometry by which paintings themselves are constructed.

If McLuhan was correct in calling art an "early warning system" for the effects of new media, then painting demonstrated that the rapid development of technical media in the twentieth century was condemning us to media navel-gazing – contemplating the workings of media instead of reflecting on the rest of the world. Or as McLuhan himself put it: "Technologies begin to perform the function of art in making us aware of the psychic and social consequences of technology." In other words, art can teach us nothing more; it has been played out. Technology is our instructor, but it only gives lessons about itself. The extramedial, or perhaps the extratechnical, has completely disappeared from the picture. Remember that painting, and literature too, are pre-industrial art forms. Those who seek to understand media effects in the twentieth century should look not at painting but at technical images.

The content of photography is the old medium of painting, but conversely the content of painting since 1839 is, to a substantial degree, photography. All postphotographic painting confronts its direct descendant. There is two-way traffic – an exchange which has been called "remediation."[16] Remediation is a depiction or imitation of one medium in another. Every medium remediates other media – preceding ones as well as successive ones. This is a law of media. The World Wide Web remediates television by means of webcams, but conversely television remediates the Web: think of the windows on news channels in which two reporters converse over long distances, floating in a vague space. After the introduction of writing, it became possible not only to write in spoken language but to speak in "literary language." The content of digital databases is made up of older media, such as written and printed text, photographs, films, video, audio and three-dimensional models. Interactive installations, in turn, work with databases to produce something that presents itself as a film, a poem or a piece of music. The letter is the content of e-mail; e-mail is the content of text messaging. At the same time, written language in letters and documents is becoming ever more compact under the influence of e-mail and its related forms.

What is new about a new medium is the way it remediates older media, but also new is the way older media remediate a new medium and thereby stay current. Everything we see or hear in the media is a reproduction of other media. All our lives we learn how to use media. One-year-olds understand what they are supposed to see in photographs and videos. Beginning with this kind of instinctual knowledge, we are subsequently able to learn to use any medium, including new ones that come on the market during our lifetimes. The experiences that we reencounter in the media, or bring with us in order to grasp what a medium is or does – such as the sense of space that enables us to look at paintings, photographs and films – these experiences are, in turn, medially tinged. When one rides a bicycle down the street, one experiences the city cinematically. Which came first: dream-as-film or film-as-dream? Every mediation is a remediation. Together the media make up one big closed system.

## Transparency and Hypermediation

There are two ways of using media to generate experience in an audience, or rather, there are two ways of placing emphasis when using media. One is to give the audience the impression of being directly connected to an actual reality – and that it is not necessary that they pay attention to the medium with which that connection appears to have been brought about. The medium then has a naturalness and does not arouse interest. Or one can give the audience the opposite impression – that of being connected not to a reality that can directly be experienced, but to a medium that generates experiences – a new, or else an ancient, medium that is still, or once more, so unusual that its mere use is unlikely and thus informative, regardless of the content. The information transfer channel can itself be informative, or it might not be. Direct connection to a reality is known as "transparency," direct connection to a medium as "hypermediation."

Transparent media create the impression of allowing the users to directly get to know the reality being represented. They hide their own existence from view as much as possible by behaving as conventionally as they can. The users look straight through these media to the "real world," without having to pay attention to the apparatus lying between their perception and what they are perceiving. "Transparency" means the medium itself is worthless, but the message transmitted through it is that much more valuable. Painting lost its transparency when photography was introduced. Photographs appear to give a less distorted image, and therefore a more direct view of the reality depicted, than paintings can. Photography is more transparent than painting. This is also why photography was considered less valuable than painting.

Something similar happens with every new medium. Again and again, new media advertise themselves as more transparent, better, more real and more complete than their predecessors, and inversely they are seen as being worthless. Film is more transparent than photography (because it moves). Television is more transparent than film (because it is live). Webcams are more transparent than TV (because there is no director). Virtual reality is more transparent than film and television (because it is three-dimensional). Writing is more transparent than the spoken word (because it endures over time). A printed text is more transparent than a written text (because it is easier to read and to duplicate). A digital text is more transparent than a printed text (because it is easier to modify and faster to distribute).

"Hypermedial" media make it impossible for us to look through them in a carefree way: they explicitly place themselves between the viewer and the viewed. They emphasize their own autonomous value in relation to the message. Their hypermediation is a result of the fact that they are either so new that there are no conventions yet for them to tacitly follow, or so old that the conventions have been forgotten. The users' awareness that they are using a medium gives them the feeling of undergoing something remarkable. The reason the Internet and World Wide Web generated so much excitement among early adopters in the early 1990s was not that they suddenly allowed the gathering of previously hidden information; it was their interactivity and immediacy. It was possible now to do more than just passively consume, as one did with books and television. And one received an immediate response, instead of having to wait for days, as one had had to with letters and newspapers.

Transparency and hypermediation are not characteristics of media, although that often seems to be the case. Rather, these terms describe sensations they bring about in their users. Transparent visual media evoke a visual space that appears as unconstructed as a reflection. Hypermedial media not only evoke a constructed, virtual space, but also show the scaffolding within which that space is built. They show not only the sculpture, but also the hammers and chisels. They show the virtual space as a process, as something that is "becoming" – not as something that "is." New media are transparent because they remediate old media. But what this transparency teaches the user is not what is unique about the new medium, but precisely what is not unique about it. Transparency is based on the recognition of one medium in another. Hypermediation, by contrast, emphasizes instead what is special, unique or new about a medium. It reveals what this specific medium, and no other, can do. What is hypermedial in a media transfer is precisely those elements we do not recognize.

Whenever a new medium is introduced, whatever characteristic of an old medium had been considered essential always proves easy to reproduce. For centuries painting had derived its right of existence from its ability to represent or evoke reality "as it really is" – and then it turned out that this ability to depict could be mechanized through the use of the camera. This forced painting to conduct a fundamental inquiry into its true raison d'être. Since photography came along, we have been unable to look through a painting to the reality depicted in it: we always see the paint. But after film was introduced, it became impossible to overlook the fact that photographs were static images. And when television came along, it became impossible not to see that everything on film was directed. From then on, films were concerned solely with the way films make us forget we are sitting in a cinema watching a projection. Once webcams came along, it became obvious that everything on television (even the news) was staged.

The transparency of a new medium is based on the remediation of a previous medium. New media reveal how awkward earlier ones were and how little their achievements amounted to in the areas where they had been considered to be superior. New media undermine old media in precisely the abilities that had been regarded as essential to them. This is why the introduction of a new medium is such a traumatic experience for loyal users of and believers in the old medium: their high Art is suddenly automated and trivialized. They experience this as the decline of civilization. The new medium does not make clear what was unique about the old, but nor does it make clear what is unique about itself – because the quality that makes a medium successful is precisely its ability to imitate the qualities of other media more easily, quickly and cheaply. To understand what is unique about a medium, we must wipe away all remediation and see what is left.

Let us again take the examples of painting and photography. The photograph was the first image to be made by a machine. All prephotographic images were made by hand. (Cave paintings appear to have been made by mouth: the painters mixed pigment and soot with saliva in their mouths and spat it onto the rock face). Traditional images are in any case directly linked to the bodies of their makers; analog technical images break this link. The difference is enormous, and reciprocal remediation is also affected.

In a painting, the painter's considerations and decisions underlie everything inside the frame, whatever it might represent. Every line, every color, is there because the painter wanted it there, or at least chose not to erase it. This is not the case with a technical image: photographers do not add or erase grains, and the picture is not based on a decision by the photographer. In this sense, technical images have no meaning whatsoever, however telling and well thought out they might be as representations. Everything discernable as meaning in an analog photograph either comes from a technical ability of the photographer (framing, lighting, focus and so on), or is projected onto the picture by the viewer, who regards the photograph as if it were a traditional image full of meaning. The power of a photograph is precisely its capacity for meaninglessness, its one-time-only quality, its mechanically realized immediacy – something that is impossible to achieve in a painting.

Paintings can imitate photographs and photographs can imitate paintings, but a photograph is always technical and meaningless, and a painting hand-crafted and meaningful. The content of photographs is painting; the content of paintings is never photography, however meaningless or "hyperrealistic" a painter might try to make his or her work. What is the content of painting in medial terms? A painting is a manipulation of matter: manipulated paint on a background creates the illusion of a spatial representation. The viewer sees paint on a surface, and at the same time a landscape or a portrait. To look at a painting is to look at an illusion. That photography has painting as its content means that it no longer manipulates matter – this skill has been replaced by the camera – but the looking-at-illusion remains. With a photograph, we are literally looking at an illusion: the illumination of the photographic plate by the light.

The difference is that photographic illusion has lost its meaning. One can understand a painting if one knows the iconography of art: symbols are depicted whose meaning can be found in reference books, in the Bible, in tradition, in contemporary art theory, in one's own experience. This symbolic and traditional interpretation imparts a meaning to painting that transcends the individual level and touches universal aspects of human life. There are no handbooks on meaning in photography, and no sense-making traditions. When a photograph attempts to have meaning, that meaning is always something cliched or stereotypical, a pointless imitation of previously seen pictures. A good photograph has no predecessors, is original, authentic and highly personal: it happens once and never again. It is because photographs have no meaning and show nothing universal that they can so brilliantly express a person's individuality – that of the person photographed or the photographer, or even the viewer.

But what is the medial content of painting; which previous medium can be rediscovered in it? God's creation of the world, or, depending on one's belief, gods' creation of the world. God, or gods, manipulated matter in such a way that our world was born. The memory of this primal event was given form by our distant (and less distant) ancestors through rituals and ceremonies. The painters of Pont d'Arc and Lascaux, and those who came later, transformed rituals into paintings by imitating the original act, and painters continue to do the same today. They manipulate matter in such a way that the world emerges from it, including animals and characters. Painting is a religious act, an act of faith, an active imitation of an act of God, or a god.

This act of painting is not itself symbolic in nature; it is much too literal for that. But it brings about something symbolic. If one looks at a painting "literally," all one sees is paint, but if one looks at the illusion, one sees symbols laden with meaning, a meaning which the creator of the painting has imparted to everything on the canvas – just as everything in the world has meaning because God created it and His hand can be discerned in it. This religious foundation of painting is why artists and art lovers can be driven to despair by the propagation of photography and later visual media. The technical image secularizes the world, actively expels God from matter, renders existence meaningless. It propagates a belief in illusion instead of in a Creator whom we can see in matter, in painting.

Photography does not create the world, as painting does; it only represents it. The virtual space of photography is a remediation of the virtual space of painting. Photography is not active or creative, but passive. This is its power, according to the classical theorists of the photographic image.[17] Such an image, they say, makes direct contact with reality by means of light entering the viewers' eye from the objects photographed through the media of lens, negative film, developing chemicals and positive printing. This is why photography can show extramedial reality and the objective existence of the world, while painting can show only intramedial reality, the painter's subjectivity rendered in paint.

This theory is incorrect: photography in fact does add something to the image it allows the world to make. This something is photogenicity. Photogenicity is a property that can be discovered or introduced in things through photography alone, and can be captured only in photographic images. It makes faces enthralling, bodies seductive, landscapes interesting to the tourist – it even gives paintings an aura they are unable to live up to. If one knows a painting only from photographic reproductions, in a museum it can be terribly disappointing.

There, it loses its photographic radiance and turns out to consist of muddy paint, sloppy brushwork, translucent canvas. The proposition that a work of art loses its aura when it is mechanically reproduced is thus also incorrect: in fact, its aura assumes staggering proportions if it is well-photographed.[18]

Photogenicity is what makes us willing to look at a photograph in the first place. Unphotogenic photographs are, and remain, uninforming. Photogenicity is the new thing about photography – new vis-à-vis traditional images and painting, but also, and in particular, new in the sense of being a newly discovered and represented property of the world. In photogenicity, the medium of photography enriches the world and the world enriches the medium of photography. Photogenicity can be found only in photography. It cannot be expressed in words, and is therefore meaningless; it cannot be interpreted, but it can be observed. Photogenicity is the poetic truth photography expresses about the world. Just look. Thanks to photogenicity, one can immediately perceive the feeling the photograph gives off, and with which all its lines and colors are saturated. Photogenicity is the part of a photograph that touches the outside world, because it is photogenicity that awakens experience in us. The experience of timelessness, of spatiality, of cheerful tragedy.

## Touch and Suspicion

The most direct form of communication is undoubtedly touch. It is difficult to lie with one's body. However often businesspeople speak on the telephone or e-mail, when it comes down to genuine trust and important negotiations, personal contact and handshakes are essential. Communication is the interpretation of feelings, one's own and another's. A glance from a man or woman can turn one's life around – from love at first sight to the sudden realization that you have made a mess of your life and urgently need to choose a different path. Seduction is almost completely based on the intensity of the seducer's feelings, not on his or her external charms. In the sphere of feelings, the greatest adventures take place through, or even in, the imagination. Feelings are impossible without imagination, because to feel is to become aware of one's physical responses to stimuli from outside. How can one ascertain whether one's interpretation of those responses is correct? Through touch: by laying one's hand on the source – the other. Touch is more than contact between skin and object or skin and skin: all the senses are involved. And biologically speaking, it is vital.

Media extend the body in space and time, but prevent touch. In place of a marvelous web of feelings and fantasies going back and forth, we get technical products and processes. We no longer look at the other; all we see is the apparatus that represents his or her face, voice or written words. There is no longer any final way of checking: the imagination becomes the only source of feelings. Once it is connected to media, the body begins to function as an autonomous entity, an information processing system. Media theory is a theory of a life without touch, a bodiless existence. A life without direct contact – in a sense, without communication. This also explains why transparent media succeed again and again by promising to be the first media not to distort perception of, or contact with, the outside world. Immediate experience of the extramedial world finally seems to become possible. Transparent media satisfy a deep desire in media users: the desire not to have to use media. But satisfaction is illusory: the extramedial is always unattainable through media, though it is the media that keep alive the idea of the extramedial.

The criticism that says experiences generated by media are not real should actually be phrased as follows: true experience is rooted in one body's unmediated touching of another. The seductive power of media lies in their suggestion that it is possible for us to become pure intensities of feeling, unhindered by the awkward bodies we have been dragging around all our lives. At the end of the 1980s there was great excitement over the concept of "cyberspace" because of its promise that soon we would be able to completely merge into the digital space of the net, leaving our bodies behind in "meat space." We would be able to feel and experience anything without physical limitations – all boundaries of sex, species, location and fitness would be erased.[19] The fact that this idea seemed highly unlikely made it all the more interesting and informative. This shows that the normality that media evoke is not a communicative sphere but a sovereign media space, a parallel world, a sixth continent of speed and immediacy in the middle of daily life.

The criticism that in media one only encounters technology and not other people can be answered with the haughty remark that one does not want to meet other people because one's self is enough.[20]

"Meat space" is "meet space," but "media space" is "me space." The term "mass media" no longer applies. Media no longer create classic crowds, human masses in which individuals conquer their fear of touch and enjoy pushing against each other in the same direction, bent on mass release.[21] Older media such as concerts, opera, speeches, plays and football matches do generate crowds, complete with cheering, standing ovations, and the push toward the stage. And very occasionally, an audience applauds at the credits of a film – but feature films actually seek to transport viewers individually. The mass support television can sometimes conjure up for a good cause or a bad war appears only in the bank accounts to which donations can be sent or as viewer ratings.

At pop concerts, bands sometimes succeed in transforming an audience into a crowd: it sings along, demands an encore, storms the stage. But otherwise, throughout the media landscape, from radio and TV to the Internet and all digital media, the point is not crowd formation but the serial creation of individual experiences: trances. And they are generated in enormous crowds of people at once; think of the DJ- and VJ-led dance events where tens of thousands of young people undergo solitary trips without touching each other, each intently revolving around his or her own axis.

According to Marshall McLuhan, the influence of media can be best interpreted with the help of the old myth of Narcissus, who fell in love with his own reflection in the water. Narcissus recognized himself in something that he was not: he fell in love not with himself, but with an extension of himself in a medium other than flesh and blood. He became anesthetized; he formed a closed system with his medium and became numb to all other external stimuli. This is true for every medium. Time after time, people become charmed by extensions of themselves in a material other than themselves. This causes not so much numbness, as McLuhan argued, but trance. A trance is a stimulation of a body from which that body can derive no consequence other than to get lost in itself. The media user, book reader, TV viewer, gameboy, techno dancer, photography fan, museumgoer, radio listener, websurfer or chatroom chatter becomes fixated on what his or her own body is doing when an influx of external energy puts it into a state which it could never have achieved or maintained on its own.

In a trance the body itself becomes a medium, an autonomous play with signs, images, impulses and vibrations: temporary equilibria, displacements, rearrangements and new temporary equilibria. A trance is a concentration on the feelings, intuitions, instincts, preferences, wishes, thoughts, smells, and memories that are passing through inside. We do not use media out of a desire for direct contact with reality, or even a need for information. We seek surrender: we connect to media out of a desire for a direct experience of something that is not ourselves. We wish to experience ourselves as we are not. Again and again, in different ways, with different media.

Painting and sculpture still possess a certain corporality. A painting is an image in which we can read an artist's touch: we can see how he or she moved brushes over canvas to bring the picture into being. A certain amount of time is present in a painting. Painting, and looking at paintings, can be compared to speaking, listening, writing and reading; all are processes that unfold in time and impose a chronological order. Speaking and listening are events, actions in time, and through them everything that is told is made into an event again. Paintings show us events in the same way. We can therefore "read" them: by moving our eyes over the canvas, we can reproduce the movements of the painter's hand. Jackson Pollock made these movements the sole content of his paintings. To read a painting is to retrace the chronological order on the canvas. Before the introduction of central perspective the passage of time was depicted in paintings, for instance, the crucial events in the life of a saint. After the Renaissance, a spatial structure – a virtual space – was represented in paintings, but the passage of time remained present in the act of painting itself.

Photography caused an unprecedented break in the pictorial tradition by severing this connection with time. The body of the person who has made a photograph is not present in the material it is made of, the photographic grains. The photographer's presence can be recognized only in the camera angle, and perhaps in the subjects' reactions to him or her (looking into the lens or away from it). In a photograph there is no time – an exposure of one-hundredth of a second is not even perceptible to the human eye. Photographs do not show events, but situations. A photograph cannot be "read"; it should be taken in all at once. In this total confrontation, the photograph delivers its blow. After that, one can study its details at leisure, but time does not exist there either, because regardless of the order in which one's gaze moves across the picture, everything is still happening – or rather, still is – at one and the same moment. Photography shows being, not becoming, as does painting. Photographs show essence, not change.

After photography, film set the photographic image in motion. This seemed to result in a new break with pictorial tradition, since two-dimensional representations had stood still for forty thousand years. Yet time is not present in film – that is, real time, actually experienced time, such as was present in the traditional fine arts. Film time is virtual time, as is evident just in the fact that film (even flashbacks) always takes place in the present. Film has this virtual present in common with dreams. Dreams, too, always take place in the now, and whatever happens, everything appears equally direct and natural to the dreamer. The nonexistence of time in the cinematic "continuous present" is apparent from the fact that great leaps across time can be edited in without the viewer experiencing any break in the passage of time.

Film, like photography, shows not change but essences: not becoming, but being. The break between photography and film is not that great. Film does not know touch either, although it tries harder than any other medium to abolish this lack of corporality by using any means permitted to cause effects in the bodies of its audience. Of all the varieties of technical image, film is the one most oriented to spectacle.[22] With television, nothing noteworthy needs to happen for days or even weeks to keep the audience switched on. But a film must captivate them from the first frame on. Film is a hot medium; television is cool.

In the 1970s, the new medium of video seemed to be becoming an autonomous artistic medium. The video screen with its wide picture lines restored a certain tactility and corporality to the technical image. If a magnet was placed on the monitor, the picture distorted into a thing with a will of its own. The point of all video art was this sort of intra-image transformation – not the portrayal of an outside world, staged or not, as with film and television. In sum: a photograph is an unmoving two-dimensional image, and the manipulation that determines what is seen in the frame takes place mainly in front of the camera, or outside the medium. Film, by contrast, consists of photographs set in motion, with an additional manipulative capacity offered by editing, which determines the order the images will appear in and how long each shot can be seen. Finally, video is film in which there is manipulation not only outside and between the images but also in the images themselves. The latter can be done by analog means, such as color correction and overlay, but today it is almost always done digitally.

Because a video image is a transparent photographic or cinematic image that has been processed, it is almost inevitably hypermedial. This made it artistically interesting in the 1970s. But the media of film, video and television quickly began to merge. Video's transformations were used to create special effects in feature films, and to make television video clips as compact as possible. The quality of camcorders became so high that video images could be blown up into film images, or broadcast directly on television: video became transparent. The distinction between film, television and video thus became artificial, or rather these categories became historic ones. Digital images no longer have picture lines, either; they consist solely of pixels. A characteristic aesthetic quality of the video image has thus been lost.

All technical images, including photographs, have now become digital. Nonetheless, while channel-surfing one can easily tell the original image types apart. It is easy to tell whether something is a feature film, a documentary, a photo, a video, a commercial, a filmed radio broadcast or telephone conversation, a remediated website, or just pure television – news, a soap or a sitcom. Television is once again totally devoted to the present. What it shows is not change but variety: the news, and every other series, shows us that there is always something new happening in the world but is unable to bring together all the fragments into one big story with a beginning, a middle and an end, as film could have. Postmodernism provided a philosophy that suited the televisual attitude to life.[23]

That technical images have no direct contact with reality – in other words, that they do not know touch – allowed them the pretense of being "objective," totally transparent. The illustrated press equated this transparency with trustworthiness. If an image had never been touched by human hands, the viewer could unquestioningly believe his or her eyes. This reversal of the normal state of affairs – in which we can only know if someone or something is trustworthy once we have touched it – cost technical images dearly once postphotographic, digital images were introduced. Now, every technical image could be changed pixel by pixel and the manipulation was not technically traceable in the final result. Light was no longer even needed to make a photograph or a film: photographic images could be manufactured purely with computer programs, through calculation. Under every photographic pixel, therefore, there lies an act of will. In digital imagery, once again, just as in painting, we see a purely intramedial reality: the image maker's subjectivity translated into zeroes and ones.

We can no longer simply believe a technical-looking image, since it might be digital. What looks like an objective reproduction could easily prove to be an artificial construction – something which, in retrospect, photographs and films always were to a considerable degree. Digital images put an end to photographic images' naive realistic claims. This naiveté, however, had given photographic images their social impact. What can you do with a photographic image that is not only hypermedial but, above all, suspect? Enjoy it and nothing more?[24] The news media can tackle the problem with the aid of their reputation: we know quality newspapers and TV channels don't tamper with their pictures (insofar as they can confirm those pictures' accuracy), and it does occasionally happen they publish corrections.

What is wrong with removing parts of a photograph or a piece of film that have no news value, anyway? It's no different than what print journalists do, after all. Isn't leaving things out the very art of journalism? And if, through sheer bad luck, a photographer has had to take two pictures where the story could have been captured in one, why shouldn't the photo editor combine the two images? Should a magazine have to print a photograph that has plenty of room for improvement simply because it never occurred to us in the past to be suspicious of technical images? These questions touch on a dark suspicion which gnaws at every use of media and disturbs every carefree encounter with them. It is an emotion that has difficulty appearing above raised eyebrows and thoughtfully pulled earlobes.

Suspicion of the media, like suspicion of art, is eternal. Despite enthusiasm about the informative and communicative possibilities of transparent media or the trance-generating potential of hypermedial media, there always comes a moment when a media user begins to wonder if his or her medium isn't hiding rather than revealing something, and making something impossible instead of opening it up. This "something" is located not outside or behind the medium but beneath it. Every use of media calls forth the vague uneasiness that what is going on in the media is something completely different than what is being claimed. Likewise, every work of art raise doubts as to whether it is nonsense, or has been made only for the sake of money or fame or to make fools of serious art lovers.

Uneasiness in the media is not directed at the propagandistic or indoctrinating use of media, or even to the power of the big media firms in the culture industry. It addresses itself to something much more elusive: an obscure, hidden "submedial space" where something is going on the finer points of which we can never know. As soon as one makes something public – thus, as soon as one uses a medium – one arouses suspicion about one's intentions. This suspicion can be neither dispelled nor confirmed. Every user of a medium secretly hopes cracks will appear in its surface one day, making visible ... what, exactly? Manipulations behind the screen?[25]

It is not difficult to achieve an effect of sincerity in media, an effect of medial truth, of self-exposure by the media. For media users believe incongruous statements and signs most of all – for instance, those that sound a common or angry note in an otherwise sensible or composed context, or a careful one amid much populist shouting. One sensible remark among a hundred empty slogans works hugely in one's favor, while one empty slogan between a hundred sensible remarks can be fatal. Submedial suspicion is an inevitable counterpart to every use of media. The emptier the signs that appear on the medial surface, the greater the suspicion that something huge is concealed behind them. Politicians who never say anything of note are probably the most dangerous of all. Adolf Hitler remains a fascinating figure, precisely because he was completely uninteresting. Or think of Marcel Duchamp's urinal and Malevich's black square: it is precisely because of their emptiness that these artistic gestures are eternally fascinating. They suggest an unfathomable profundity.

What does all this teach us? If the medium is the message, then that message says that we must believe in the media (or that we must not). As soon as one gives up one's belief in media, however, it is not suspicion which takes over (that is part of the medial belief system), but astonishment. One connects to a medium and the strangest things begin to pour out. As long as one stays connected to a medium, one forms a closed system with it, as one must if one wants to do justice to oneself and the medium. We are not victims of the media, but nor are we their rulers. The point is to translate the world of experience into the world of a medium, and in such a way that translation back to the world of experience is possible. The media do not make up the world, but a world. What we call our world, too, is one world among many, one space among many. Striving for a sensible use of media always means living in multiple worlds at the same time, because this prevents medium and user from remaining a closed system. In doubling oneself, one does not become an open system; one becomes pure wonder – that is, a system connected to other systems. One becomes a system of feelings and thoughts that organize oneself and others: feelings and thoughts that had been unknown until one found one's medium. This makes art possible.

# Historical Media Theory

## Introduction

"The major advances in civilization are processes which all but wreck the societies in which they occur."[1]

To the question of what keeps human history going, three answers have been given: humanity, economics, and means of communication. According to the first view, humans organize their lives with the help of two factors that afford stability and one factor whose aim is instability and development.[2] The stable factors are the state and religion; the unstable one is culture. The state is the expression of human political needs, of our desire for an orderly life in which justice prevails and community life and individual existence can develop. Religion is the expression of human metaphysical needs: the answer to the question of why we would want to live orderly lives, develop ourselves and let others develop. Both of these factors can persist more or less unchanged for centuries, even millennia; little would happen in history were it not for the third, unstable factor: culture.

Culture is an expression of the spontaneous human urge to keep trying, discovering, and making new and different things. This creative impulse is also the factor that is able to criticize the state and religion and breathe new life into them when they threaten to become empty forms. Every period in history can be characterized in terms of these three factors. Sometimes the state has the upper hand; at other times religion does; at others, culture. Sometimes art is subordinated to religion, and sometimes to the state, but conversely, religion and the state can be undermined by art, or else elevated to great heights by it. This view of history allows a clear categorization of all historical periods, but its drawback is that it neglects to explain one thing: why humans are creative. That we are spontaneously and naturally creative is not an explanation but an admission of ignorance: only behavior that cannot be accounted for by the two other explanatory factors of state and religion is termed spontaneous.

The second explanation for the progress of history says economics is the driving force. There are two schools of thought here. According to the first, it is humans' innate competitive drive that makes us repeatedly come up with new ideas in the desire not only to support ourselves and our families but to have interesting lives while doing it.[3] The "invisible hand of the market" repeatedly prompts inventiveness and new ideas in enterprising types, since otherwise the competition will run away with their market share. When the rest of the world is rushing forward, whoever isn't moving forward is going backward; and the world is rushing forward, for wherever there is anything to get or swindle someone out of, an entrepreneur shows up in due course, looking to make a profit. No ideological system can resist the market, for ideologies prescribe behaviors people would never spontaneously or naturally engage in, such as showing solidarity, sharing and sharing alike, according equal rights to all, respecting traditional values, and taking responsibility for the world and distant posterity. According to this view, only the market – that is, the urge for self-actualization through self-enrichment – is spontaneous and genuine.

The second school of economic explanation sees things differently. Naturally, the economy determines which desires and needs can and cannot be satisfied, for without money nothing is possible. Wealth, however, is created using means of production which lie in the hands of a relatively small group, the ruling class, but the labor necessary to create that wealth is supplied by the working class, which has nothing but its brute strength and the inescapable need to sell it in order to earn a living. Because the drive to compete compels people to invent and use more and more new means of production, there arise more and more new forms of exploitation of labor by the rulers, and this is what is known as History. Ideologies, culture and religion are means of blocking this harsh reality from view and making it tolerable – they are forms of false consciousness. No one is free: the "winners" must compete; the "losers" must allow themselves to be exploited.[4]

The two schools of economic explanation, in brief, complement each other: one describes the view of the ruling class, the other that of the workers. But neither explains why humans can invent the wheel one day and a telescope the next, or found a new science, or introduce a religion, or bring fine art or literature into blossom. In practice, economics seldom comes first: usually, something is invented to begin with and only afterward is a profitable application sought. The idea that economics is the engine of history, then, also fails to answer the question of where human creativity comes from.

The third view of the driving force behind history points out that everything for which communication is necessary – politics, religion, economics, culture – depends on media. Without means of communication, nothing would happen, since even if something did, no one would know about it, and even if everyone did know, they wouldn't be able to talk about it. Media are the source of all creativity, and of all power. Every large political, economic or religious structure struggles with the balance between exercising power over space and exercising power over time: that is, the balance between the size of the state or domain and the length of time it can continue to exist. Some empires pursue maximum size and soon disappear – Alexander the Great's, Genghis Khan's, Adolf Hitler's – while others expand and contract and last for an astonishingly long time, like the Roman and Byzantine empires. This view has it that the factor disrupting the relationship between "space" and "time" over and over is neither the restless, creative human spirit nor an innate or learned competitive drive, but the invention and distribution of new means of communication. These undermine existing power structures and make possible new power monopolies. Power not only tyrannizes and restricts, it also stimulates and inspires: it is not only oppressive, but also productive.[5]

One could also formulate the preceding as follows: every medium has its own tendency ("bias") toward either time or space.[6] In the 1930s, Hitler chiefly used the medium of radio, whose waves did not stop at any political border, and which allowed him to reach Germans all over Europe and exhort them to support the Reich. Hitler established one of the biggest European empires in history, but it lasted less than five years. The medium of the Byzantine Empire was parchment, which is expensive and difficult to write on but lasts for centuries, and that empire lasted a thousand years, though for part of that time it covered half of Europe and at other times it was no bigger than the city of Constantinople (Istanbul). In any empire, state or religion, the means of communication lie in the hands of a relatively small group, an elite which, surprisingly, does not have political power itself, but serves those who do as their advisors, teachers, officials, journalists and intellectuals. This group determines what is and is not allowed into the culture. The introduction of a new medium in a society inevitably leads to power shifts and the ascent of a new elite. A recent example is the PC: it made techies who had previously been considered geeks into a programming elite, and in barely ten years, the few big hard- and software firms that employed them became the most powerful companies on earth.

Time after time, "human" creativity, inventiveness or restlessness arises out of the coupling of humans with media. Only through media can we discuss, remember, think, reconsider, monitor, change, or discover something truly new. Media are not just means of helping individuals to achieve unforeseen feats: each medium also evokes its own environment or mentality which penetrates as far as politics, economics, culture, religion and psychology. The introduction of a new medium in a society starts a process of reorganization which changes humanity as much as it does the society, but the medium that brings about all these unanticipated upheavals, shifts and new structures is changed, too. Once established, the new social order becomes the normality, and it can last for centuries if the medium's "bias" is aimed at permanence – on the condition that no new media are admitted. A "ruling medium" can create great stability across space and time. The most stable medium of all is the spoken word in oral cultures, ones without writing: some of these have existed for a hundred thousand years.

The media-theory version of history begins with oral cultures. In cultures without media, people live in "acoustic space": prehistoric space in which they are totally oriented to hearing, and not vision as we generally are, simply because they have no writing or other visual media (beyond a few decorations and magical cave paintings). In oral cultures, everything in the environment is perceived immediately and synchronously, for the ear basically hears everything at once. In visual cultures, people look at individual objects and mentally reconstruct the separate perceptions into a process of cause and effect. For residents of acoustic space, all causes and effects, all relationships between objects and processes, take place at the same time. They have an "integral awareness" of the world around them; everything is linked together in the same moment, not step by step as it is in the visual worldview, which is ordered through written and printed language.

We experience the difference between acoustic and visual space when we arrive in the city after a long stay in the country or the wilderness. The noise level in the city is crushing, and the number of stimuli coming through from all sides, even inside one's home, is punishing. The only way of surviving this assault on the senses is to switch over from an aural orientation to a visual one. Little sound penetrates visual space; it is as if the ears develop "lids" like the eyes. Those who have grown up in the country and move to the city experience this shut-off as an amputation of the most important of the organs that make them human: free contact with the outside is disturbed, the core of existence is affected, and the senses become the greatest enemy. Yet under such conditions it is the senses that can offer salvation. If one learns to "read" the city like a text, and instead of allowing information to penetrate all at once takes it in bit by bit, as if reading a book word by word, one will, after a bit of practice, succeed in creating a new order, not only in the environment but also in oneself. One is a different person in visual space than one is in acoustic space. One returns to one's acoustic self when one is back in the country – it takes a few days – and returns to one's visual self again as soon as one is back in the city.

Media history is the story of the transition from ear to eye, from a wild culture to a civilized one, from a culture based on hearing to one which is becoming ever more visually focused, from a worldview in which everything forms a whole to one in which, through human effort, fragments are cemented together into a whole. Below, I will tell this story from the linguistic point of view for Western cultures. Slowly but surely, the spoken word imposed a structure on acoustic space. Written language subsequently restructured that worldview from a mythical one into a rational one. And when the art of letterpress printing was invented, reason went a step further, and developed into the natural and human sciences – the final victory of visual space over acoustic. With the spread of computers, this process took a further turn – the direction of which I will discuss below.[7]

When a new medium appears, older media do not simply vanish into nothingness along with their accompanying environments, mentalities, normalities and habit formations. Instead they disappear slowly, and only partially. In our own era, there are traces of every medium that has ever existed, traces which have been called "survivals" (*Nachleben*): persistent habits and customs that have lost their purpose but continue to exist as folklore, routines, decorations, cliches, superstitions, astrology, games, sayings, styles, taboos, or just pointless uneasiness.[8] Anyone who wishes to be "modern" always wages war against these survivals in an attempt to purge the latest medium's environment of any old – and in particular old-fashioned – taints. But survivals are also outstanding means of getting a grip, in our era, on the experiences of distant ancestors who lived with, and shaped their world through, different media than ours. These old worlds are not gone forever: they live on, undiminished, in everything we do without thinking, everything that makes us a tiny bit ridiculous but that much more recognizable, and that much more charming. In the empire of media nothing is ever really gone for good.[9]

# Spoken Language

## Acoustic Space

The first syllable ever spoken by a human being contained the most meaning of any sound ever: it referred to everything. We will never know how the apes who moved onto the plains and drifted from southern Africa into the north after drought set in began to speak. Evolutionary theories about the larynx dropping, the vocal cords developing gradually or by leaps, and the prefrontal lobes of the brain becoming active are as convincing as is the idea that language came from the imitation of animal sounds because that was the simplest way of referring to the creatures in question.[10] It is also possible that a meteorite hit the Gobi Desert one hundred thousand years ago and a virus from it spread over the earth, causing not only the development of the ability to speak but also a great urge to mate in certain anthropoids, a combination which helped the speaking apes to multiply like wildfire and, thanks to their superior communication abilities, to massacre all other anthropoids of similar stature in the fight over the available sources of food. "Language is a virus from outer space."[11]

The first words were gods.[12] This explains the curious fact that in many languages some words are feminine and others are masculine: some words originally stood for goddesses, others for gods. Language and myth arise together; the myths provide a narrative, evocative explanation for the power of the words. In the first phase of this developmental process, everything in the world is thought to be pervaded by an indeterminate power or energy. This power has been given names such as mana, manitou, wakanda, orenda, and mulungu. This first form of religious thought makes no distinction between living and lifeless things: everything has a soul. Mana does not change, but nor does it stand still. It concentrates here and there, creating sacred places charged with "numen" – divine energy – and lowering the religious intensity of the rest of the world. The sacred places sometimes form paths through the landscape, giving it a particular structure, with some places that are taboo and others where one can act more freely – though it might, for instance, remain forbidden to urinate in such a way that one's genitals are revealed to the sea or the moon. Trails past sacred places allow people to orient themselves in the landscape and become walking and trade routes.

At specific locations where mana has concentrated, at a certain point in time humans begin to identify gods – temporary and local ones, for instance in one special oak or alder in a clearing. A whole mountainside can even be a god. A god can also manifest itself in certain actions performed by humans, such as throwing gazelles' bones to predict the future, or in the utterance of a certain word, which thus functions as a blessing or curse. A god can also speak through the voice of an oracle. In this second phase of religious thought, the sacred and the profane become separated: at certain places and times, one is overcome suddenly by a feeling of awe, fright, wonder, or gratitude, and one knows that a god or goddess is nearby. Nothing special is taking place elsewhere. In this phase, gods are always people, individuals with their own names.

Slowly but surely, after this period, similarities between individual "special" gods are discovered, and a third phase of religiosity begins. Characteristics of the specialized gods are combined to make up universal gods with many different names. Thus Zeus, Hera, Apollo, Artemis and the other deities of ancient Greece had whole series of titles according to the regions where they were worshipped, the times of year, and the needs of the populations. This is the phase of great, complex mythologies, in which epic poets and bards try to weave together all the myths that have been passed down in a poetically acceptable way and adapt them to the requirements of the day (see box opposite page).

This third phase rarely ends peacefully. When northern tribes invaded Greece at the end of the Stone Age, they conquered the local peoples by subduing their gods – usually by discovering and appropriating those gods' secret names. A vanquished tribe's god's name was then appended to the name of the victors' deity. Centuries later, the Bronze Age tribes, in turn, were conquered by invaders from the east and south and underwent a defeat comparable to that which they had inflicted on their predecessors: they lost their gods' names to the invaders' gods and saw their own culture swallowed up by the oppressors'.

It is possible to trace the history of the invasions in Greece, and later the conquest of Ireland and Wales by tribes which had been driven out of Greece and northern Africa, through deciphering the gods' names and the jumble of myths concerning the relationships between the gods and stripping them of all the inversions, distortions, rationalizations and smokescreens inflicted by the conquering tribes' singing historians. The most important inversion was the changing of the main deity's sex: if originally she had always been female, then in the tran-

### 700 B.C.: Hesiod on the Golden Race

Golden was the first race of articulate folk
Created by the immortals who live on Olympos.
They actually lived when Kronos was king of the sky,
And they lived like gods, not a care in their hearts,
Nothing to do with hard work or grief,
And miserable old age didn't exist for them.
From fingers to toes they never grew old,
And the good times rolled. And when they died
It was like sleep just ravelled them up.
They had everything good. The land bore them fruit
All on its own, and plenty of it too. Cheerful folk,
They did their work peacebly and in prosperity,
With plenty of flocks, and they were dear to the gods.
And sure when Earth covered over that generation
They turned into holy spirits, powers above ground,
Invisible wardens for the whole human race.
They roam all over the land, shrouded in mist,
Tending to justice, repaying criminal acts
And dispensing wealth. This is their royal honor.

From: Hesiod, *Works and Days* and *Theogony,* translated by
Stanley Lombardo, Indianapolis/Cambridge 1993.

sition from matriarchy to patriarchy she was made male. From the old songs it is possible to deduce the highly secret names of the singing bards' own tribal gods, provided one is prepared to reason as poetically and cryptically as the old poets did – and this leads one to discover that Judaism and Christianity are just reworkings of much older beliefs concerning the preservation of the movement of the seasons and the cyclical fertility of the land and the animals.[13]

In this third phase of religiosity, language acquires a characteristic which we so take for granted that it can only surprise an extremely elevated linguistic consciousness. How is it possible that we can look at a certain tree in a certain place and recognize this completely unique and specific object as "a tree" instead of as a unique and specific living thing? How is it possible that our experience of concrete objects and people is so abstract that we can give them general names? Even if one is able to determine that a given tree is a plane or a maple, this specific designation is still amazingly universal. And yet language would not be possible if we did not perceive in this abstract way – though the opposite proposition seems likelier: that perception would not be possible if language were not so abstract. The abstraction of reality is so deeply rooted in the human brain that it takes place during or in perception itself – if occasionally we succeed in breaking through this routine and seeing something or someone as a unique object or an extraordinary person, it leads straight to religious awe, aesthetic emotion, and love.

Language and myth not only arise at the same time but develop together. To a mythical consciousness, everything is connected to everything else, but language fragments this experience and then assumes the function of cobbling the connections back together somehow or other.[14] And thus the days of the week are associated with the sun, the moon and the five planets visible to the naked eye, but also with seven sacred varieties of tree and, later, with seven letters of the alphabet that spell the secret name of the god – and those letters in turn are used to determine the layout of temples, sacrificial places and megalithic monuments. Every plant or animal that is important for food, medicine or religious aid is given a name and linked with a taboo for a specific day of the week or year, a person, a bodily state, and so on. And thus patterns and structures arise, creating not only a more or less orderly world for gods and people, but also an increasingly abstract vocabulary, through which this "science of the concrete" can be transmitted from generation to generation. The mythical mentality does not deal in theoretical explanations of cause and effect, but in analogies between phenomena. One does not see logical connections in the world, but similarities and differences.

In the fourth phase of religious thought, all the greater gods' individual characteristics combine into one god: the best known of these are Jahweh or Jehovah, Elohim, God, Ahura Mazda and Allah. In monotheism, all numen is concentrated in one single deity, one word. Here and there numen can still be experienced in nature or social life, but it always refers directly or derivatively to the single god which dwells in the center of organized religion, in the temple, synagogue, church or mosque. Even Protestantism, which requires a personal bond between God and its believers, does not allow them to turn their backs on the church in order to experience that bond undisturbed in the open air. The single god always imposes a moral regime on the faithful: a closed world in which a struggle is taking place between good and evil. To maintain this regime, there must be a form of organization that presents the choice starkly week after week, repeatedly demanding that the choice stay clear and pure, but also allowing for payment of penance and forgiveness of transgressions.

There is a fifth phase of religiosity. In it, religion lets go of the link to language, and the divine can be experienced only as that which is fundamentally inexpressible. In contrast to the first phase, when everything on earth is pervaded by an indeterminate power, now a very definite power can be felt behind or beyond everything, a universal creative energy. Brahma is one name for it; prana and tao also fall into this category. It is a power which manifests itself in the field of tension between the world and the self. The ultimate goal of fifth-phase religions is to experience unity between the self and the world – atman and brahma. In the West, this phase can be found in the negative mysticism of people like Meister Eckhart, who argued that one could only love God "as no one." "God is simple ground, silent wilderness, simple silence" – "His nature is that he is one nature." In this phase, every believer struggles with the paradox that while everything is one, or nothing but oneness is real, the world meanwhile stubbornly continues to consist of separate parts. The problem is that there are no longer any words or even images for this religious feeling, and it can therefore only be described negatively, as everything it is not – and this while in this phase we usually have a word for everything on earth.

This final form of religiosity is not the inevitable consequence of the developmental process that starts with the beginning of language. We can trace a process in mythical knowledge by which people become conscious of the images that knowledge uses to give coherence to the world. Mythical consciousness then realizes it is mythical, laying open the possibility that it could become something else. This more abstract consciousness can then turn into a wordless adoration of the divine, but it can also transform into a different sort of knowledge – a kind of knowledge or thought which does not tinker with images of concrete objects, relationships and feelings but formulates theories about them. On the one hand we can use these theories to test reality for regularities, but on the other we can also use reality to test the theories themselves for internal consistency and tenability. Philosophy and modern science arose out of this way of thinking. They demanded that thought contain no contradictions, and also that it not be at odds with practice.

To conclude this section: in our dealings with the world we acquire two kinds of knowledge.[15] The first is called "discursive," because it can be directly articulated in words and concepts ("That's an oak tree; that's a horse") and arguments can be constructed with and about it. Discursive knowledge is the kind of knowledge sought by philosophy and science. But there is also a second kind of knowledge which cannot be immediately captured in concepts because it is still too new and unfamiliar. This knowledge is therefore defined with the aid of images, pictures and metaphors. This knowledge is not discursive but "presentational" in nature. A metaphor or presentational image has a meaning, but one which for the moment can be expressed solely by means of that single image. It is impossible to say what exactly the image stands for, because there are not yet any other examples to stand for the same thing; no distinction can be made between image and meaning. An eagle can serve as a symbol of state power because both the eagle and the concept of state power exist, but originally there was only the eagle, and then it was sensed that it in some way or other corresponded to the leader. A presentational image is different from an illustration, which is representational in nature and has an unambiguous meaning.

Discursive insights are logical and rational; presentational insights are mythical and irrational, part of the "natural religion" whose various phases are described above. Both insights occur simultaneously in one and the same person, community, school or institution, without being found internally contradictory or even disturbing. There is no such thing as a purely mythical consciousness or a "primitive mentality" which approaches everything irrationally or prelogically. No primitive peoples have walked the earth for at least twenty thousand years.[16] The mythical approach, even today, is used with phenomena for which no normal explanation can be found. The rational explanation eventually found for practically every phenomenon proves time and time again to be a logical reconstruction of an originally mythical description.

Everything that is completely different and falls outside our discursive worldview appears to us first as a god or goddess, a miracle, something overwhelming, a mystery, a brush with the Other. This metaphorical experience shows us that our rationally ordered worldview has its limitations but that these can be broken through from outside, for the world is forcing an insight upon us which exceeds and reorders all our knowledge. We can use the new metaphors that present themselves for these experiences in writing, art, architecture, politics, whatever. As we do so, we formulate the new knowledge in such a way that it becomes graspable, applicable in the everyday. It is no longer unique but usable in ever more areas. And thus it becomes part of logical, discursive thought and common sense, and loses its religious flavor. It leaves the domain of mythical approach and expression, and what had originally been presentational knowledge becomes discursive forever. From then on, it is open to philosophical and scientific testing.

What does a mythical metaphor, a presentational expression, actually stand for? Its content is a feeling. A plain, a cloud, the edge of the woods, an eagle, bones thrown into the air, a sacred place, a holy act, a curse or a blessing is just one more image for a feeling that cannot be expressed in words, but is no less real and demanding for that. The god is an emotion first, a story only later. Without feeling, without that underlying layer, every story remains a free-floating fantasy. Storytelling in the mythical sense of the word is an attempt to express something that forever escapes us, until in all the telling, writing, hearing and reading we achieve enough distance from what occupies us that we can not only see it before us but also understand it in a nonmetaphorical, discursive language. At that point, we can discuss the relevant insights without undermining our own existence in the process. Criticism replaces animosity. When the faithful are asked what exactly they believe in, they get tongue-tied (or name the creed or denomination they belong to). Nonbelievers need not believe in the mythical insights they have acquired – even if these make up the foundations of their existence. Mythical, religious, or artistic knowledge is completely different from, but equivalent to, scientific and philosophical knowledge. Myth and art explore and explain the world as it exists in our experience. The sciences explore and explain the world as it exists independently of humanity but nonetheless knowably.

## Myth as the Art of Memory

Words, but also pictures and music, can be used in two ways: as signals and as symbols.[17] When we hit our finger with a hammer and shout a swear word, it is a symptom of the fact that we have hurt ourselves. To be sure, the cry is a word – "Dammit," say – but it is not intended to indicate anything except the presence of pain. Art as self-expression – for example, poetry as an expression of emotion – makes signals of the signs through which it is brought about, that is, signs indicating the presence of certain feelings or thoughts in a poem's creator. Music intended to make its listener cry, or dance, or rage, also consists of signals: signs that the audience should do something. We need not think about signals: they are spontaneous expressions and call for spontaneous reactions.

Symbols are not spontaneous, nor do they demand spontaneity from us: they are constructions, and they require reflection. A signal is directly connected to both the sender and the receiver – we see a dog and say "Doggie"; we see a child steal a cookie and say "No!" A signal has a fixed, obvious meaning which is often apparent just in its intonation. A symbol, by contrast, has an indirect relationship to what it denotes: we talk about a tree when there is no tree in sight. We talk about pain without feeling it at the time. We consider the pros and cons of certain rules of conduct without worrying about their implementation. We act out cheerfulness or gloom on stage. Or we act as if something flat – a painting or a photograph – has depth. While signals are means of expressing and evoking experiences, symbols are means of thinking about experiences instead of simply undergoing them. Popular culture works with signals; high culture works with symbols. The symbols of art are words, sounds, materials and media. The meaning of symbols cannot be deduced from observation or reason; it must be learned from people who use them. A symbol can be expressed in different languages, and in different ways in one language, and still retain its meaning. When there is no one left to explain what a symbol stands for, it becomes a mystery forever.

When a poet writes a deliberate verse or a lively one, he need not be contemplative or high-spirited himself, as long as he employs language in such a way that the resulting poem gives shape to the feeling of melancholy or joy, so that the reader can think about it – discursively or presentationally. A poem either works or it doesn't, and what works about it is something intangible – that is to say, non-discursive – something located on the mythical metaphorical level described above. Gloom, gladness and all the thousand other feelings a poem can exude are experiences consisting solely of words strung together by the poet to have a rhythm, a rhyme, a cadence and an irregularity that combine to make clear exactly which sorrow or joy the poem is about. A poem can also evoke an argument – that is, the experience of argument (what the argument is about is less important). Literary prose, too, describes not events but merely the experience of them – in contrast to scientific and journalistic texts, which do manage to represent the outside world, regardless of whether certain things can be experienced. Poetry, and literature in general, are means of expanding, deepening and refining the reader's range of experience. Poetry is about virtual life, virtual experience: that is, feelings evoked by a poem which have no direct cause outside the poetry itself. A good poem about a child should move us not because children are sweet, but because the poem is constructed to make us think about our feelings for children and the emotional value of words. Why is the word "washcloth" so moving in a poem?

The distinction between signal and symbol is an important aid in understanding the function of poetry in oral cultures: that is, cultures in which the spoken word is the sole means people have of sharing stories, memories and thoughts with their contemporaries and passing them down to their descendants. These cultures are the oldest on earth – they are prehistoric, for history begins with the introduction of the written word. In oral cultures the spoken word is the only carrier of a tribe's or region's archive. "Word" must be understood here in a broad sense, for in oral cultures there actually are no words – individual words are not experienced as clearly defined units. If you ask an illiterate person to name a word, he or she will respond with something a written culture would call part of a sentence, or a line of poetry, or even a whole song. Without writing, it does not matter whether something is a word, a clause, a sentence or a song – there are only groups of sounds that inextricably belong together as cognitive units. Grammar as a method of analyzing sentences and words, too, only becomes possible with written language, in written cultures.

Two kinds of language act exist in oral cultures: normal conversation, whose function is mainly social and whose content may be quickly forgotten, and exceptional speech, whose purpose is the storage of information. In oral cultures, poetry exists to make language memorable. Rhythm, meter and rhyme are incomparably strong mnemonics, certainly when accompanied by a harp, a lyre or another musical instrument. Even today, we can often sing along with a song we haven't heard in twenty years as soon as we hear the melody – even in a language we cannot speak. Language that contains no rhythm or other physical anchor goes in one ear and out the other. An explanation for this is that our brains work rhythmically: brain areas do not follow a fixed innate rhythm (like the clock inside a computer) but are constantly busy synchronizing with each other. In doing so, they often orient themselves to some rhythm in the environment: a ticking clock, our steps as we walk, or the keys we strike while typing.[18] A good way to calm a restless baby is to provide it with an external rhythm by patting its bottom.

Metrical poetry is one such means of achieving synchronization in the brain, and it promotes memory significantly. Non-rhythmic prose is almost impossible to remember. For this reason, it is appropriate to call poetry the oldest human language. The earliest kings spoke in verse, simply because if a leader pronounced his orders without rhythm they were quickly forgotten. Yet speaking with too much regularity doesn't work either: the brain is constantly busy interpreting rhythms, and as soon as it succeeds, they disappear from consciousness, and seep back in only when an irregularity appears. "The real life in regular verse is an irregular movement underlying."[19]

Oral cultures existed in the Middle East between 60,000 and 3000 B.C., after which writing arose, together with the great states sited in what is now Iraq and Iran. The epic of Gilgamesh as it was passed down in cuneiform on thousands of clay tablets is a written edition of an originally oral epic poem. Myths always have predecessors. In Greece, around 1000 B.C., at the time of the Mycenaean civilization, there appeared an early script called Linear B. It was a "syllabic" form of writing: the characters stood not for letters but for syllables. In practice, Linear B was ambiguous and vague, making it unsuitable for bureaucratic and literary purposes, and it disappeared after a short time. When Homer composed his *Iliad* and *Odyssey* in the eighth century B.C., he did it entirely from memory – there was no writing available around the Aegean Sea at that time. This fact makes Homer's work a gold mine for the study of idiom in an oral context. Longer epic poems did arise in the "Dark Age" of ancient Greece, but they were either less interesting than Homer's work and thus quickly forgotten, or not regarded by later editors as worth the effort of preservation, or else incorporated by these editors into their edition of Homer's work in the second or third century B.C.

The first Greek poet to write down his work was Hesiod (seventeenth century B.C.). He had a new form of writing at his disposal, the classical Greek alphabet, which had been derived from the Phoenician alphabet in the previous century. Hesiod's *Theogony* is still at the boundary between oral and written culture, because the poet borrowed the basis for the poem from itinerant "rhapsodists," or improvising popular storytellers. His *Works and Days* was the first poem in the Western canon to be composed in writing. Because of his borderline position, Hesiod is a rich source for research into the difference between the oral and written uses of language. A third important source of knowledge about orality is the Yugoslavian heroic poets, who recited their work until late in the twentieth century, being illiterate (or actually analphabetic: in the context of written culture, oral culture is known as analphabetism). In the 1930s and 1940s, thousands of LP recordings of performances by these poets were made in Serbia and Bosnia-Herzegovina, and afterward put into writing.[20] This research was intended to solve the "Homeric question": that of whether and how Homer composed his work.

Oral language, for lack of a better term, has a number of notable characteristics that differentiate it from the written word. Rhythm and cadence have already been mentioned – rhyme occurs less often in longer works but plays an important role in ballads. In addition, oral language is always concrete. Abstract concepts are not used, for they are nearly impossible to remember (this is still true today; we soon forget theory if we do not keep it up); concrete language, which is directly related to the perceptible world or derived from practical language use, does stay with us. Oral language is also always visually evocative, full of comparisons, which can be lengthy. In addition, it is used actively, to describe events, developments and processes rather than final states or ways of being. Thus, in an oral culture, one would say, "That mother bore that son," rather than "He is that mother's son": the first describes an active process, the second a passive state. Also noteworthy are the many, often word-for-word repetitions and parallellisms that appear in any given story, and the traditional use of language, full of standard expressions and set word combinations. Oral language does not seek to be authentic or original, but conventional, and this is precisely why it is an effective medium for information storage.

What an oral poet tries to achieve in reciting a poem is a direct emotional influence on his listeners. Oral poetry is a hot medium: it affects the audience not only through language, but also through inflection, tone, facial expression, gestures, touch, even the way the narrator smells: almost every sense is played on. We cannot really call it recitation, for the poet has not learned his oeuvre by heart but has picked up standard expressions – "formulas" – and set combinations of events – "themes" – since childhood through witnessing performances by other oral poets. Subsequently, he has slowly but surely developed his own expertise in molding and combining formulas, themes and corresponding gestures (see box opposite page). As he performs before an audience, the oral poet combines standard expressions and set series of events again and again into a story with which he must somehow or other hold the interest of the audience, whose reactions he notices immediately.

Here is an example of such a theme: a king is sitting with his knights around the castle dinner table when a message comes. A galloping horse has been seen on the horizon. The messenger on the horse brings news of an enemy invasion of the kingdom – or else, say, an invitation to a wedding. One of the knights at the table might lose his temper – another theme – and launch into a tirade, leading to a duel or an expedition to right some injustice. The journey that follows this beginning, to the wedding or the injustice, is itself made up entirely of subsequent themes, such as the stopping place, the welcoming reception, the peculiar overnight stay, and so on. Time and again, a moment occurs in the story when the poet can choose a theme, and he bases that choice on the audience's reaction. This makes every performance, every

# The Education of an Oral Poet

In order best to appreciate and to understand the process of composition that we call oral, and thus to eliminate our prejudice against the "illiterate" singer, we must follow him during the years which he devotes to learning the art. If we take our future oral poet in his unlettered state at a tender age, let's say fourteen or fifteen, or even younger (singers tell us that this was the age at which they learned, although they usually mean by it only "when I was just a young boy"), and watch him learning the art, we can understand what this process is.

We can trace three distinct stages in his progress. During the first period he sits aside while others sing. He has decided that he wants to sing himself, or he may still be unaware of this decision and simply be very eager to hear the stories of his elders. Before he actually begins to sing, he is, consciously or unconsciously, laying the foundation. He is learning the stories en becoming acquainted with the heroes and their names, the faraway places and the habits of long ago. The themes of the poetry are becoming familiar to him, and his feeling for them is sharpened as he hears more and as he listens to the men discussing the songs among themselves. At the same time he is imbibing the rhythm of the singing and to an extent also the rhythm of the thoughts as they are expressed in song. Even at this early stage the oft-repeated phrases which we call formulas are being absorbed.

One of the best accounts of the learning process is to be found in Parry Text 12391 from Seco Kolic. As a boy he used to tend sheep alone on the mountain. Here are his own words: "When I was a sheperd boy, they used to come for an evening to my house, or sometimes we would go to someone else's for the evening, somewhere in the village. Then a singer would pick up the gusle, and I would listen to the song. The next day when I was with the flock, I would put the song together, word for word, without the gusle, but I would sing it from memory, word for word, just as the singer has sung it [...] Then I learned gradually to finger the instrument, and to fit the fingering to the words, and my fingers obeyed better and better [...] I didn't sing among the men until I had perfected the song, but only among the young fellows in my circle *(druzina)* not in front of my elders and betters."

Seco here roughly distinguishes all three stages of learning; first, the period of listening and absorbing; then, the period of application; and finally, that of singing before a critical audience.

From: Albert B. Lord, *The Singer of Tales*, Cambridge (Mass.) 1960.

recitation of a "poem," different. There is no "original" version of the poem, but rather a cloud of themes that materializes each time into a unique recitation.

The "oral" audience is no more capable than the oral poet of distancing itself from what is being told; distance from language becomes possible only with the introduction of writing. As long as only the spoken word exists, language is part of the body and directly affects it. In this sense, oral language is purely presentational. It consists entirely of signals, though those signals are not spontaneous so much as traditional. The tradition is not a fixed canon of sacred texts and folk tales but a living tissue of formulas, story fragments and themes, plus a tremendous rhythm, which a poet must combine in such a way that the audience hangs on his every word. The audience wants to hear the same story over and over again, though any part of it can be changed if the social, cultural or political circumstances alter. This, by the way, holds not just for an oral culture's poetry but also for its laws: because these are recorded nowhere except in the memory of the upholders of the law (the elders of the society), they can easily be adapted to new circumstances while allowing everyone to feel as if they are ancient and venerable. Only with the introduction of writing does it become possible to act according to the "letter of the law," instead of the "spirit of the law," as is always done in oral cultures.[21]

The nice thing about oral cultures is their flexibility. Because no original versions of the laws or the stories of gods and heroes exist, no breaks ever occur in these cultures, and they can continue to exist for thousands of years "unchanged" in the minds of the bearers of culture, and nevertheless be completely different at the end of that period from how they were at the beginning – there is no one who can check, for no documents have been passed down. In addition, an oral poet can give two renditions of a story that differ greatly when heard on a sound recording, and still stubbornly insist that he has performed the same poem twice. This is because he remembers meanings, and thus symbols – that they are phrased differently each time is immaterial. A recitation of a poem can be better on one evening than another, because a spark has leapt between poet and audience and made the language take flight. It is never better because the source text was repeated more accurately, for there is no source text. In oral cultures, originality is ineffective and therefore inappropriate. Unanticipated remarks can only be understood through reflection, and reflection is something that is hard to do when a poem is being composed as it is recited, or recited as it is being composed. And yet oral poets are different from each other, for each one can recombine, embellish, shorten, lengthen, or add a twist to the mass of stories and poems in his own way.

In his two masterpieces, Homer proceeds in essentially the same way as any other oral poet – including modern ones. His language is always concrete, evocative, active and conventional. He piles formula upon formula and combines one series of themes with the next – though he does so in his own magnificent way and with such an economy of resources that the work remains highly inspiring even today. We read Homer as a poet of fierce passions and inevitable fate, drawing on ancient myths that might stem from events of hundreds or thousands of years earlier – but once recognized as an oral poet, he comes across as an encyclopedist who sought not only to move his audience with his work but also to document the knowledge of his people and his time.

For this is what all that traditional poetry and song was for. Epic poetry is the only means oral cultures have of recording the knowledge they have amassed over time about facts, rules of behavior and skills, albeit in an unstable or in any case variable form.[22] At the beginning of the *Iliad*, for example, Homer depicts the argument between the Greek king Agamemnon and the great warrior Achilles over the question of who should receive which portion of the spoils from a raid. Every human emotion makes an appearance, but at the same time the audience is learning how rulers are supposed to behave toward their subordinates, their slaves, and in particular their equals; what a ruler's rights and obligations are; which rights and duties citizens have toward their leader, wives have toward their husbands and vice versa, et cetera. And the description of Achilles' shield is a catalog of manual skills, as is the description of the Greek fleet, and so on and so forth. Homer's poetry is a strong example of the mythical "science of the concrete" mentioned above.

The performance of oral poetry is an example of edutainment: learning for fun. Because the audience identifies with what it hears – if the poet is any good – it naturally acquires the encyclopedic information it is told and goes on to apply it as a matter of course. For every situation in daily life, there is a story, which is not so much imitated as lived. A myth, as preserved in formulas and themes, is not a tale about the past but a timeless story that is actualized again and again in the present. The myth prescribes a model for the present, keeps the present liveable by offering an appropriate convention for every situation. People heard the knowledge repeated in poetry from childhood on, and the code of behavior that followed from it became, as it were, built into their bodily movements. There was no critical distance between knowledge and the knower; this would arise only with the introduction of writing. The myths that have been passed down to us through the tireless work of later editors are not symbols for a deep, old, esoteric knowledge; they were once signals for how life should be lived in a culture that knew no writing and had to make do entirely with hearsay and word of mouth.

The characters in myths were archetypes: everything that had ever been done was attributed to them. Because it was impossible to remember everything every individual had ever done or to know who had first performed every deed, similar acts were ascribed to a single individual – Gilgamesh, Hercules, Odysseus, Oedipus, Beowulf, Arthur, Charlemagne or Mwindo. Such a figure thereby became surrounded by a group of stories, themes, motifs, proverbs and formulas, out of which the oral poets composed the epic poetry with which they illustrated to the society how one ought to behave in a Hercules-, Odysseus-, Oedipus- or Arthur-like situation. Or, to be more precise: how, given the situation, one could become a Hercules, an Odysseus or an Arthur. The "oral" individual does not experience him- or herself as a sovereign person or an autonomous unit, but as part of a living, animated world, as part of a tribe or people or tradition, and as serving a god. The oral individual is a system that follows the rules, taboos and stories of the group, without needing or being able to subject those rules to discussion. As long as a system organizes itself so that it can retain the information necessary for this self-organization, there is no need for criticism, theory or explicit ethics. Doubt is something that arises with writing. It is impossible to look at oneself from outside without an external medium, and oral language is internal – it stays inside the body and inside the group.

# Written Language

# The First Writing

Writing was invented independently at three distinct places and times, in Mesopotamia, China and Central America. It is thus an example of convergent cultural evolution: a development leading from strongly different points of departure to the same result. This suggests that not only spoken language but writing too was inevitable once the first apes had drifted onto the African plain.[23] The human brain underwent a rapid evolution after spoken language was introduced or invented about a hundred thousand years ago – five thousand generations – but this complex brain only became fully conscious after the appearance of the human technique of writing, which not only revealed what language was but was also used to speak and master it. The ability to read and write apparently leads to neurological changes, though unfortunately research on this matter is still in its infancy. It has been discovered that a considerable reduction in the number of synapses in the brain takes place around age five or six, when children usually learn to read and write, but how and why this happens is still unknown.

The oldest known form of writing developed, step by step, in the fourth millennium B.C. in Sumer, in what is now southern Iraq. It was a pictographic script, and it spread in three directions, to Egypt, Elam (in western Iran) and the Indus Valley, assuming a different form in each case. It is a mystery how and when Chinese logographic writing – which eventually came to have fifty thousand characters for words and concepts – and the syllabic writing of the Mayans in Central America arose, although it is clear that it was after 3000 B.C. The twenty-four-letter Greek alphabet did not appear until 700 B.C., as a distant derivative of the original Sumerian script. Each time this script was used for another spoken language, it prompted the abolition and adoption of more characters. By about 1500 B.C. this had developed into an initially northern Semitic, and later Phoenician, vowelless alphabet. If Sumerian writing and its early derivatives had only characters for concepts and a few syllables, this Semitic alphabet was the first purely phonetic writing: the letters referred directly to the sounds that made up the spoken language.

The first vowelless alphabet – derivatives of which are still used in Hebrew and Arabic – was transformed around 700 B.C., in what was then the Greek part of Turkey, into one with six vowels (represented by Semitic characters that stood for sounds that did not occur in Greek). Unlike the Semitic languages, Greek, an Indo-European language, contains words that consist entirely of vowels, or begin or end with them. Written words that sound practically the same can have completely different meanings – contemporary English examples are "bed" and "bad." Uniquely, the Greek alphabet contains character combinations for sounds that are pronounced differently than the combination of letters with which they are written: for example "o" and "u" for an "oo" sound. These sounds can be identified as mental objects only after analysis and abstraction of the spoken and written languages. This ancient Greek alphabet metamorphosed via the Latin alphabet into the twenty-six-letter "English" alphabet, in which you are reading this book.

A form of writing was not adapted to a new language after an analysis was performed to determine whether the respective sounds and connotations of the writing and the unwritten language were the same. Through transcription, people came to realize their own languages had characteristic forms which differed from those of other, older languages. Only writing can render visible a spoken language's structure and construction. An already existing script is a matrix which is, as it were, pressed onto a new collection of data – a spoken language which has no writing yet – revealing that there is a good deal of data that does not fit in the matrix. It is this matrix, the older written language, which makes differences visible. Writing teaches its users to see their language differently, or rather to see it in the first place. They suddenly discover that their language consists not only of words but also of syllables, and even letters. Who could have guessed![24] By no means every written language is an alphabetical language, by the way, and fewer than one in every ten languages spoken on earth is even converted into writing by its users; only a hundred languages are used for literary purposes. The alphabet is not a universally applicable form of writing: for a great many languages – such as that of the Bushmen, with its "unalphabetic" clicking sounds – it is a hopelessly clumsy vehicle. The missionaries and ethnologists of past centuries who wrote down all manner of spoken languages in alphabetic script simply did not know how else to deal with them.

The emergence of the earliest writing can be seen in archaeological finds from temples, storage spaces and graves in the Near East. Great numbers of small clay objects from the period between 8000 and 3000 B.C., some bearing scratches, are often found on digs there. Initially these were thought to be trash and cleared away, but then it was realized that these items contained information: they were media. They are known as "tokens" – symbolic objects.[25] The very oldest kind, used for 4,500 years, have simple, geometric forms: cones, spheres, flat and lenticular discs, cylinders, tetrahedrons (pyramids), ovoids, rectangles, triangles, double cones and hyperboloids. These tokens were easy to make: a ball of clay, of which there was an abundant supply around the Euphrates and the Tigris, was formed into the desired shape with the fingers and then baked in a small oven. Around 3500 B.C., "complex" tokens began to appear in new shapes: paraboloids, bent coils, ovals and rhomboids. There were also realistic shapes – miniature tools, furniture, fruits, people, dishes and animals. Also new were the many markings on the tokens: single and parallel lines, cross-hatchings, stars, squares and various punctures. These tokens took more manual skill to make than "simple" ones.

The very oldest tokens, from 8000 B.C., were all found in early, more or less permanently inhabited farming villages of round huts in Iran and Syria. Until 3500 B.C. these simple tokens spread to various residential areas, including caves and nomadic encampments, but mainly to permanent small cities of right-angled houses. Complex tokens have been found only among the ruins of later cities with monumental architecture, such as Uruk in Iraq, Susa in Iran and Habuba Kabira in Syria. They are often found together in great numbers inside official buildings, and hardly ever in residences. Many have also been found on waste heaps, indicating they were discarded after use. In sum, the appearance of simple tokens is associated with the emergence of sedentary agriculture (which replaced Neolithic hunting and gathering), while complex tokens are found in buildings that – as the seals and weighing instruments discovered there also make evident – belonged to the bureaucracy in the large cities, which were led by priest-kings.

Simple tokens thus probably refer to farmers' products, while complex tokens represent goods produced in the city. A number of simple tokens, such as cones, spheres and discs, stood in early prehistory for non-standardized amounts, such as "a small basket of grain," "a bigger basket" or "a granary" (comparable to non-standardized amounts in modern recipes, like "a cup of sugar" or "a little water"). With the emergence of religious and political bureaucracies starting in 3500 B.C., these amounts became fixed. From then on, a short wedge-shaped token stood for an exact amount of grain – a "ban" – and a circle for an amount six times that, a "bariga." Characters representing numbers of animals also appeared: a lenticular disc stood for "a herd," a disc for "ten animals." The complex tokens, with their lines and notches, indicated specific kinds of things: instead of "animals in general," one could now indicate that one meant male sheep of a certain age and size. There were also complex tokens for new products such as perfume, rope, metal and bracelets. Amounts of goods had to be kept track of because they were part of the sacrifices made to temples and taxes paid to kings – tokens showed how much of each thing remained to be delivered. A token measures debt, something which is not there (symbol), and not merchandise, which is present and which can be measured by money (signal).

From the beginning of the fourth millennium, tokens were archived in two ways. They were either drilled through and tied together with cord, or stored in a clay container, a hollow ball or other shape closed with a seal impressed with the owner's stamp. These containers, or "bullae," are a crucial step in the development of writing. They were used primarily in temples between 3500 and 2600 B.C. From the outside of a bulla one could not tell what was inside – this could only be checked by breaking the sphere, which would destroy the seal bearing the owner's stamp. So bookkeepers marked each bulla's contents on its exterior, by pressing the tokens into the clay before putting them inside. It was not long before they began drawing the tokens' contours on the bullae with a stylus, sometimes because the clay had become too hard to press the tokens into it, more often because the complex tokens with all their lines and cross-hatchings did not transfer well.

This led to the next step in the process. There is not much point in putting tokens inside hollow spheres if one is already marking them on the outside and no one is ever going to look inside; the marks alone are enough. But why then maintain the spherical form? And so it was that around 3500 B.C., people began to use flat, pillow-shaped clay tablets with token imprints on them, and the actual tokens disappeared from the accounting system. A crucial development quickly followed, although those who carried it out did not realize what a historic step it was. Within barely two hundred years, eight generations, all token imprints had been replaced by characters inscribed with a stylus: pictograms that mimicked the original shape of the tokens with their lines and cross-hatchings. While markings on bullae had been signs of the tokens inside, pictograms inscribed on tablets were actual symbols for absent tokens. This change signified a definitive step in the direction of writing. A three-dimensional sphere became a two-dimensional circle; a disc with a hole, two concentric circles; a cylinder, a rectangle – and these pictograms soon began to get more abstract and easier to draw. What had started out as concrete objects became abstract signs, pictograms that referred to something other than themselves, that is, the old tokens from the accounting system. The earliest writing, in short, was not a reproduction of a spoken language but a remediation of an older medium, the token system.

Numbers were initially indicated in a very direct way: if one wanted to make a note that three pitchers of oil needed to be delivered, one pressed the token for "pitcher of oil" (an ovoid scored once across) into the clay of the bulla three times. On the tablets, this system was replaced by pictograms indicating abstract numbers. Instead of making the mark for oil pitcher three times, one made two marks: one for "three" and the other for "oil pitcher." The sign for "one" was a short wedge shape, derived from the sign for a small amount of grain. Two through nine were the same mark repeated two to nine times. Ten was a circle, the sign for a larger measure of grain. Sixty was a large wedge, 600 a large perforated wedge, and 3,600 a large round mark. A mark that had originally stood for a concrete amount of grain was thus given the additional meaning of an abstract number; in this way, symbols became signals once again.

This practice which had begun as a bookkeeping method developed in two directions. On the one hand, it led to a pictographic notation system, which would turn into cuneiform after 2700 B.C., when the syntax of spoken language was adopted so the characters could be put in an order that could express more than bookkeeping data. This was the first fully written language. On the other hand, the method also developed into a notation system for numbers. The tokens formed the basis for geometry (which was derived from their shapes), but also for algebra (the specific tokens for numbers). The emergence of writing, in sum, coincides with that of mathematics. Every theory that assumes the content of writing is the accompanying spoken language are at odds with the facts, and this has been true since the very earliest writing. Only with the appearance of the Greek alphabet did a one-to-one relationship between written and spoken language become possible. The phonetic alphabet with vowels and consonants was the first writing to directly represent a spoken language, but it arose more than two thousand years after the first written language and was just one more in a series of remediations of it.

"New concepts produce new consciousness."[24] Quite a few new concepts arose during the process just described, which between 8000 and 700 B.C. led via tokens to cuneiform and the alphabet. The Near East has been inhabited by humans for 600,000 years, but the oldest symbolic objects that have come down to us date from 60,000 to 25,000 B.C. Pieces of ocher have been found in caves; ocher was not functional but was probably used to paint the body (indicating consciousness of corporality). Flowers and antlers have been found in graves; these were also nonfunctional and thus probably symbolic (indicating humans' consciousness of their own mortality). And bones have been found bearing rows of parallel notches; these are the oldest artifacts found in the region. The notches might have been decorative or magical in nature, but more probably they constituted a lunar calendar: bones were a place to record observational data concerning the moon. Bones, then, are the oldest known attempted method of recording and transmitting information in the region.

If these notched bones were a medium, they incorporated three new concepts. First of all, they were a way of translating concrete and specific data – observations about the movements of the moon – into abstract and non-specific marks. Second, the information was removed from its context: the phases of the moon could be kept track of separately from weather conditions or the social status of the observer. Third, knowledge was separated from the knower. It was stored in a cool medium (notches on a bone), not passed on in a hot one (oral poetry). The new "consciousness" which resulted from these new concepts was a far-reaching objectivity in the way information was handled.

The farming communities that began to use tokens around 8000 B.C. were the heirs of an ancient symbolic tradition. They were still scattering red ocher in graves and putting antlers in the foundations of houses, but they were also making the first animal sculptures; the oldest known animal drawings from the region date from 15,000 to 12,000 B.C. And they introduced something completely new, a new kind of symbolic object, an entirely new medium for storing and transmitting information: the token. Each token had a specific meaning: grain, beer or oil; a small, medium or large amount. In this way, tokens differed from notched bones: the notches had no unequivocal meaning but could be used for every possible kind of information, like tallies.

In all probability, tokens were hierarchically organized on the bookkeeper's table – for example, the largest at the right and the smallest at the left – and this hierarchy was reproduced on the bullae and in the way tokens were threaded on the cord. In this way the tokens acquired a relationship to each other, and a rudimentary syntax arose. The tokens' precision made them an ideal basis for what would later become pictographic writing. The tokens formed an external memory in which an endlessly large amount of information about an endless number of goods could be stored, without the human memory running the risk of becoming overburdened in the process (this is the disadvantage of Chinese writing, which no one can remember in its entirety, although every character can be looked up in the dictionary).

Many new ideas were embodied in the token system. Every token had meaning and conveyed information (semanticity). Each had one unique meaning (discreteness). And each was always reproduced exactly in order to preserve that meaning (systematization). The token system consisted of a large number of elements which could be combined with each other – for example, a token for a crop and a token for an amount (codification). The repertoire of tokens could be expanded without limit once the rise of cities made this necessary (openness). The shapes of the tokens did not depict what they stood for, but were randomly chosen (arbitrariness). Closely related token forms could refer to meanings that had nothing to do with one another (discontinuity). Tokens were signs for things and amounts, not words (independence from spoken language). Tokens were classified and used according to a number of precise rules (syntax). And tokens referred solely to information concerning real goods (economic content). It was not until after 2900 B.C. that tokens were remediated into pictograms, and thereafter into cuneiform; and only with pictographic writing were historical and religious texts written that fell outside the scope of economics.

With the transition from the token system to pictographic writing around 2900 B.C., a number of new concepts appeared. Unlike tokens, which were chucked onto the trash heap after a while, pictograms retained their meaning whatever the circumstances (preservation of information). Tokens could be used to link different kinds of information: for example, a name could be added to the characters for "ten sheep" to make what amounted to "Kurlil's ten sheep." Digits and numbers replaced the one-to-one reproduction of quantities used in the token system. And phonetic possibilities arose. The first step from pictographic to phonetic writing was made when people felt the need to register individuals' names on clay tablets more precisely and began to do so using symbols for various things which, when read phonetically, produced the intended name, as in a rebus. In the course of the step-by-step progression from tokens to mathematics and written language, there arose a new way of looking at and understanding the world, but also a new way of experiencing oneself in that world.

## The First Self

Written language is a cold medium: it addresses only one sense, the eye, unlike spoken language, which speaks to the whole body. In literate circles, efforts to enhance the effect of speech, such as facial expressions and gesticulations, fall out of use, and the spoken word is eventually presented as neutrally as is written language. In written cultures, everything revolves around meaning – that is, the discursive meaning of language – and the presentational or emotional side of language is preferably dispensed with. It is quite amazing that spoken language can be converted into letters that can be understood by others, especially considering how much is lost in the process: all the nonverbal signals people use to let their conversational partners know whether an utterance should be understood as serious, ironic, sincere, false, convinced or noncommittal. The tones of voice people use to divine each other's meaning, even when they do not share a common language, are absent in writing.

The notion that spoken language is the content of written language is incorrect, even for phonetic alphabets. Various devices can be used in written language to conjure up the illusion of speech, but in general the two scarcely even share syntax. In spoken language, precision and lack of ambiguity are unnecessary, for the speaker's intention always comes through, or if it does not the listener makes that apparent. This is true even in telephone conversations, where a host of clarifying signals are absent. In written language, meaning must be transferred entirely through words and their order, aided as necessary by punctuation marks and typographic devices such as underlining and capitalization, and, in print, italics and boldface. There is no response from the reader, and the writer thus finds out only long after the writing process whether what he or she has written has actually come across. In oral cultures, meaning is embedded in the body. In written cultures, it is located in a mental space behind language.

That written language is distinct from spoken language is evident in the fact that the first written language, Sumerian, was made up of pictograms that did not prescribe pronunciation but referred to concrete objects and relationships. For this reason, it was able to spread across a region in which dozens of different dialects and at least two main languages, Sumerian and Accadic, were spoken. Numbers are contemporary examples of characters that do not prescribe pronunciation; this is the reason today's numbers are used worldwide, and by machines. Sumerian writing evolved slowly but surely into a phonetic written language, in which the characters did denote sounds. Around 1500 B.C., the first major literary texts were being written in phonetic Sumerian, but by then, surprisingly enough, the language itself was no longer being spoken anywhere – it had become a dead language. Cuneiform was taught only at special schools for clerks and officials, who learned to write on practice tablets, large numbers of which are still being found today at archaeological sites. There are other examples of written languages without oral equivalents. For instance, theologians and scholars have been writing and reading in the same Latin language for more than fifteen hundred years, while in a parallel process, the language developed in southern European countries into the various Romance languages as we know them today. Scholars' Latin came to be used exclusively by men, and the same was also true of rabbinical Hebrew, classical Arabic, Sanskrit, classical Chinese and the Greek language of the Byzantine church.[26]

Precisely because written language is separate from spoken language and in this sense autonomous, it is outstandingly well suited for rendering a spoken language's structure and operation visible and knowable. In written language, words are literally separate from the world outside language: they obey only the syntax of the language to which they belong. When words are used to describe relationships and events in the outside world, this can be done in any number of ways: there is no necessary or fated connection between words and things. In an oral context, however, words inextricably belong to the thing to which they refer. A person's name is a characteristic or a part of his or her body. This is why a person's name can be used to call down a curse or blessing: to misuse someone's name is to abuse that person, and to hallow someone's name is to bless him or her. With the introduction of written language, a distance arises between the word and the thing, between the name and the person. Writing therefore put a virtually immediate end to every form of "word magic."

Written language is a sphere unto itself, existing not only alongside spoken language but also alongside material reality. The abstract, immaterial, "mental" character of written language has major consequences for the consciousness of the literate. Writing detaches knowledge from the knower. Written knowledge is something one can look at, criticize, deconstruct, reorder, or improve from a distance. Contradictions we do not notice in the oral transfer of knowledge suddenly become disconcertingly visible once we write that knowledge down. The logical analysis of discourse quickly leads us to the insight that much, not to say nearly all, written language is, if not senseless, then at least inconsistent or vague – as twentieth-century analytical philosophy observed. Only trivial statements, it turns out, can be logically consistent and true. The only informative utterances are those that are improbable and therefore fly in the face of logic. This insight was applied by the modernist poets, whose work in writing and print deliberately avoided every link to spoken language, and in doing so became sovereign, absolute, or else fragmentary. And these are just the effects of written language on knowledge – the effect of written knowledge on the knower is at least as amazing. All knowledge turns out to belong to someone, to the one who knows, and thus to an individual, in place of the community of storytellers and listeners who were responsible for the preservation and transfer of knowledge in the oral culture phase.

Written language no longer need be poetic to be remembered: it is fixed in an external memory such as a clay tablet, a roll of papyrus or a paper book. Rhythms and cadences, mythical adventures, active and concrete language, rhyme and alliteration – all these can be jettisoned. Even in poems, things are possible now that were not in the days when poetry was an edutainment medium. Thus a poem can immediately be identified as non-oral if it contains enjambments – that is, if a sentence can run over onto the following line, instead of each line being a complete sentence, as was necessary in oral poetry for people to tell where the lines ended. Prose arose with writing. Boring books arose with writing.

But so did stories full of subtle detail, sophisticated thought, summaries and theoretical considerations of the cultivation of plants, as in Hesiod's *Works and Days* – stories full of things which have no place in oral poetry because they are too difficult to remember. What we know as "oral poetry" – the Gilgamesh epos (passed down in cuneiform), Homer (ancient Greek), the Hindu Vedas (Sanskrit) – is in fact a hybrid of oral and written literature, for in writing it down the editors were less concerned with making the language flow acoustically than with making it visually manageable.[27] This is even more true for books of "myths and legends of primitive peoples," many of which were published in the twentieth century: some writers made myths into literary masterpieces, writing them down as compactly as possible, and omitting everything that made them typical oral poetry.

The emergence of the alphabet around 700 B.C. in Greek Turkey did not lead to the rapid and comprehensive education of the Greek population or the elite – on the contrary, the introduction and propagation of writing, first to the Greek islands and from there to the mainland, was a long process in which the early adopters had to overcome much resistance, as they do at the introduction of any new medium. Even in the fifth century, in the golden age of Athens, when the philosophers and the tragic and comic poets were writing the works that are still read today as pinnacles of Western civilization, only 10 to 20 percent of the population was literate. The rest were still living in an oral culture. In the two hundred years between 700 and 500 B.C., the alphabet was used mainly to write down oral poetry – not so much to save the works for future generations as to make it possible to verify whether students had memorized them correctly. This is the beginning of the end for an oral culture: once there is a single "standard version" of a poem, improvising a poem while one performs it is no longer possible, and the living tradition ossifies into folklore.

The Greek "pre-Socratic" philosophers, such as Heraclitus and Empedocles, were among the first to develop their thoughts while writing, not yet really as prose but in the form of the powerful statements and slogans the older oral art still reverberated with. They wrote with reed pens on rolls of papyrus, which had been imported from Egypt to the Greek world since 670 B.C. As they worked, these early thinkers ran up against the problem that the concrete language they had inherited was not especially suited to the articulation of abstract ideas. In oral language, one can describe changes, but not the concept of change-ability, as Heraclitus tried to do. He does not describe change as a process, which would have been the oral approach, but rather inquires into the principle of it – one level of abstraction higher, one might say. His statement "panta rei" – "everything flows" – is an example of this. It takes one more level of abstraction before this becomes "changeability," but Heraclitus did not take that step. In their aphorisms the first European philosophers felt obliged to contort the syntax of oral Greek in all sorts of ways in order to write down thoughts and insights to which the language had never before lent itself. This explains why their writings are so obscure and fascinating. Only in the fifth century B.C. did written language become developed and independent enough that Plato was able to write about abstract concepts in accessible Greek – although his work also remains difficult to translate into the kind of "literary," "printed" or "electronic" language into which we are in the habit of shifting our thoughts.

With Plato, the effect of alphabetic writing on its users' view of the world and self-image comes to light with great intensity. Plato translated the medial environment called forth by the alphabet into a political platform, although paradoxically enough the books in which he did so are written in the form of minutes of conversations between the philosopher Socrates and mostly young members of the Athenian elite. Plato's language contains words which do not refer to processes nor to the principles behind them, but abstract those processes and principles into universally applicable concepts. Thus he points out that all kinds of rapid and slow change have a timeless and eternal side: the underlying concepts of "speed" and "slowness." Likewise, the concept of "size" or "scale" underlies all large and small things. The concepts of speed and size are absolute, however relative the phenomena they describe might be. Plato's concepts refer, as he himself puts it, not to "becoming" but to "being," not to coincidences but to eternal truths.

In the area of morality, too, Plato does not describe events and adventures to illustrate just and unjust behavior, as Homer does. Instead he writes about justice as an independent, substantial thing. Justice is not a divinity as it is in Homer – Plato recognizes only one God, to whom he gives no specific name. For him, justice is something that is, rather than something that is done – an abstract notion, a theoretical concept, an idea (also called form). Plato was not a philosopher who thought up and developed various new concepts so much as the first philosopher to start to think in concepts in the first place. Plato invented conceptual thought as such. And for "thought," "writing" would actually be more correct.

One reason Plato allows Socrates to speak in conversation is that in classical Athens there was little reading, and accordingly much talking. Education was provided by itinerant teachers – the Sophists – and was completely focused on oral tradition. People learned to read only after adolescence. Until Plato's publications, books were no more than reference works for looking up existing knowledge; they were certainly not the authentic expressions of original minds. As a qualification, it should be mentioned here that the oldest known written poem, Hesiod's *Works and Days* – while it is, to be sure, a typical reference work – opens with a personal note from the author explaining why he has written this poem full of farming facts. Hesiod had had words with his brother Perses, whom he considered a sluggard, and wished to show him what a farmer would do if he knew how to get down to work rather than going around looking for trouble. The first written poem thus reveals more of the poet's individuality than anything the oral poets ever composed. Homer does talk about "me," but we learn little about him except that he exists. Hesiod is a specific person; he has a "self" in the recent meaning of the word.

In his writings, particularly in *The Republic*, Plato wages war against the Sophists and the education system, because they teach the old oral knowledge while a completely different kind of knowledge is available that far exceeds the old poetic wisdom and platitudes. Like many new-media users, Plato appears to have been unaware of the fact that he owed his new insights to his new medium – he was mainly aware of the failings of the old medium, oral poetry. And he attacks it viciously. Classical Homeric poetry is bad for growing children, for it is full of sordid stories of murder, incest, adultery, senseless violence, abuse of power, and contempt for those above us – even the gods are a motley bunch who screw themselves silly and randomly support first one side and then the other.

Mythical poems full of injustice and nonsense could still have had a moral function, if not for the fact that they aimed entirely at identification, or "mimesis," as Plato calls it. Oral poetry was purely sensational; the reciters as well as the audience entered completely into the events of the story, allowing themselves to be stirred up rather than calmly reflecting and learning wise life lessons, as they would have in Plato's education. Real knowledge, according to Plato, is not mimetic but "descriptive": it shows us the world from a critical distance, and it is verifiable, clear, reasonable and true. Poetic knowledge is unverifiable, confused, irrational and illusory. Descriptive knowledge is consistent and free of internal contradictions, unlike mythical knowledge, which is dominated by a principle of this-one-minute, that-the-next. Knowledge, however, does not become consistent by itself; the knower must be trained to make it so. What Athens needed was not schools in which the old excitement was maintained, but academies where a higher philosophical way of thinking was taught (see box at end of chapter).

For Plato, alphabetic writing was a transparent medium, and the oral tradition was hypermedial. He saw and rejected the specific characteristics of the old medium, and he simply did not see the existence of the new medium of writing. We cannot blame Plato for having a poorly developed media awareness, for he found himself confronted with a change in his self-image, which must have made him extremely happy, but also extremely grave. Plato knew he had discovered his soul thanks to his escape from oral culture. Writing revealed the eternal absolute truth of the ideas or forms that lay behind the phenomena of this world, in a mental domain that could be accessed only by those who renounced the short-sighted physical excesses and blindnesses oral culture was prone to. Plato could only see this domain which lay behind writing by looking through writing itself.

In oral cultures people do not ascribe their own reactions, plans and desires to themselves but to some voice or power which acts on them from outside. Homer shows his heroes doing this over and over: Penelope begins weaving a shroud for Odysseus "because a god in my lungs breathed that I should do so" (usually translated as something like "because a god inspired me to"). Agamemnon excuses his barbaric behavior towards his fellow captains in the Greek army by saying a voice from outside – a god's, he assumed – told him to act that way. The Homeric heroes did not have anything like a moral or psychological "self." To Homer the word "psyche" still meant "life in general."

For Plato, however, "psyche" meant "inner life." The psyche is the part of us that thinks, and can make moral decisions and acquire scientific insights. It is the seat of responsibility, an infinitely precious thing in nature's kingdom. In an oral context, no one considers himself an autonomous subject or distinguishes between the thinker and the thought. What modern people experience as the "self" is for people in oral cultures part of the cosmic life force, mana, divine inspiration or an enemy's curse. But if Plato wanted something, it was because he himself had decided to want it. Plato's doctrine of the autonomous psyche is the counterpart to his rejection of oral culture. Plato saw that the written did not coincide with the writer, that the writer was separate from what he did, that his psyche was separate from what he thought. Plato was one of the first on earth to sense his own self.[22]

How is the self brought into being through writing and reading? People in oral cultures are certainly capable of some degree of abstraction, given that they can sense perfectly well what others mean by what they say. Tone, emphasis and non-verbal signals are carefully picked up and interpreted. This explains the bizarre answers people from oral cultures give on tests administered by researchers from literary cultures. In a study into the logical reasoning ability of "pre-logical" subjects, for example, literate researchers said, "Imagine that everything on the moon is blue. If I bring back a rock from the moon, what color will it be?" Very few oral subjects said "blue." Most gave evasive answers, along the lines of "I've never been there"; "People say all sorts of things about it"; "Why would you bring back a rock from the moon?"; "The rock would be white like the moon"; and so on. The respondents were unable to tell from the researchers' tone how the question was meant – as a joke, a trick question, a request for information or an invitation – and so they tried to challenge the questioners a little further before giving an appropriate answer.

This "testing" or "tasting" of intention is a first-order met-alinguistic act: in oral cultures people know there is a difference between what is said and what is meant. Writing, though, makes possible a second-order metalinguistic act. One reads something and determines for oneself what its intention or meaning is – this is still a first-order act – but then one also determines that this assumed intention is just an interpretation: other interpretations are possible and might be correct, and one's own might be wrong. The interpretation says less about the writer than it does about the reader – the reader determines the meaning of what is written, not the writer. Consciousness of one's own subjectivity arises with this second-order act. There is an authority present in the reader that oversees his or her reading behavior. Listeners in oral contexts have no internal observer of their listening behavior, since listening is totally aimed at immersing oneself in and familiarizing oneself with the events in the story. The first-order act is found in all cultures and is thus universally human; the second-order one occurs only in written cultures.

## 400 B.C.: Plato on Poetry

The very best of us, hearing Homer or one of the other tragic poets copying some great man in grief, running on and on in his outcries, or wounding himself in his pain, have feelings of pleasure and let our hearts go out to the picture. We give ourselves up to it and praise, as a great poet, whoever makes us do this most.

We do.

But in our own lives, when some grief comes upon us, we take pride in the opposite behaviour, in our power to keep quiet and take it with courage, believing that this is a man's part and that the other we were praising in the play is a woman's. Are we right to praise so what we would be ashamed of in ourselves?

By Zeus, no. There is no reason in that!

There is if you look at it this way.

Which way?

In our grief there is that in the soul which is kept back by force, which by its very nature is in need of tears and lamentations as an outlet. This is what the poets please and delight in us. And what is best in us, having never had a right education or even training, lets down its guard over this grieving part because here we are looking on at the grief of others. But what we have pleasure in when we see it in others will have its effect on ourselves; after feasting our feelings of pity there it is hard to keep them down in our own grief. Few are able to see that.

Most true.

And it is the same with the causes of laughter, with comedies, or in private talk. When you take the greatest pleasure in things so low that you would be full of shame about them if they were yours, you are doing just what you do as the tragedy. Sometimes you let yourself go so far that before you know it you become a clown your-self in private. And so, again, with the desires of sex, and with anger and all the other passions and desires and pains and pleasures of the soul that go along with all our acts. The effect of such poetry is the same. It waters and cares for these feelings when what we have to do is dry them up. It makes us be ruled by the very things which have to be ruled, if we are to become better and happier men.

I may not say no.

Then, when the praisers of Homer say that he was the educator of Hellas, and that if a man is to guide and better his behaviour he will do well to give himself up to reading Homer, and that we are to order our lives by his teaching, we may love and honour these peo-ple – as doing their very best – and agree that Homer is the highest and first of all tragic poets; but let us keep true to our belief that only hymns to the gods and praises of good men may be allowed in our state. For if you let in this honey-sweet music, pleasure and pain, not law and what may rightly be thought best, will be its lords.

Most true.

From: Plato, *The Republic,* edited and translated by I.A. Richards, Cambridge 1966.

# Printed Language

## Fathers of Science

It might seem odd to think that self-awareness is a consequence of writing and reading, and some derision was heard when the proposition was first put forward. Yet the theory says no more than that humans are creatures who bend to their will not only the landscape in which they live but also their own inner selves. Through the use of external technologies, people are capable of discovering and/or calling into being internal abilities which they could not possibly have known they possessed before those technologies existed. The existence of these technologies was not planned, nor were their psychological and cognitive effects. And this regularly arouses the suspicion that technologies such as writing, reading, and the next step in the process, the art of printing, are inventions that created themselves via humans. Don't technologies bend us to their will rather than the other way around? And what secret cosmic plan is behind that? It was the introduction of the computer that did the most to increase suspicion (or else enthusiasm for the secret plan): "Mankind is a catalyzing enzyme for the transition from a carbon-based to a silicon-based intelligence."[28] But suspicion of technology is probably as old as the first stone axe or straw basket: whenever there is a new technology, some people worry that this is the one that is going to definitively take over and reduce humans to slaves, robots or machine parts. In practice, however, people become smarter and smarter the more technologies they have at their disposal, for we are as intelligent as we manage to make our environments. A high school student in our time knows more than Leonardo da Vinci did. One could also say: to get by in our time, one must process much more information than one would have had to in the early Renaissance, and be accordingly more intelligent.

Along with the submedial suspicion of secret plans, every new medium fosters the feeling that immortality is now within reach. This happens because the new medium is free of that which makes people so preeminently human: the awareness of mortality, the certainty that one will die. The alphabet had scarcely been introduced before Sappho of Lesbos wrote, "Although they are / only breath, words / which I command / are immortal." Written language can do precisely what speech and song cannot: continue to exist. With the arrival of the personal computer and the Internet, there arose the science fiction subgenre of cyberpunk, full of fantasies of the human mind emigrating to cyberspace and leaving the mortal body behind. The computer can do what the body and mind cannot: be everywhere at once. With the arrival of the printing press, people initially believed they would be able to give immortality to all the forgotten classical and occult writers whose un-findable works had suddenly become readily available. After that, they believed they would be able to make their own loved ones immortal by singing of them in verses that would be reprinted into eternity, instead of having to be laboriously learned over and over again by heart or copied out with all the accompanying danger of an incorrect render-ing.[29]

Throughout the Middle Ages, people both derived intense joy from the medium of writing and wrestled with its characteristic effect, which was that the meaning of what was read seemed to be located in a men-tal domain behind language. Written language describes a part of real-ity that cannot be seen with the eye: its conceptual content. Every new medium calls forth a new form of virtual life, an illusion which allows us to explore a previously uncharted part of the spectrum of human feeling. In this newly discovered inner realm there could lie a way out of the trap that awaits every living creature: mortality. In the Middle Ages, the customary manner of understanding a text – usually the Bible or a work of a Church Father – was to let what had been read sink in until a light went on and its secret, allegorical, moral and perhaps occult meaning was revealed to the reader. No written sentence was meant to be taken literally: the point was always to discover the spiri-tual meaning behind the writing. In fact, medieval readers did not have the slightest idea what a text's literal meaning might be: for them, there was only the revealed spiritual meaning. This is still true for inex-perienced readers, who suspect all sorts of profundities in texts which upon literal reading prove to amount to little – as one sees when one rereads a literary discovery of one's youth after twenty years. Reading what is there is a skill acquired only through long practice.

    Throughout the Middle Ages, the habit of mainly paying attention to what was happening behind the text – in one's own head – led people to copy books according to meaning, as one does when translating from one language to another, instead of transcribing them word for word. The result was that almost every text that was passed down was corrupt, insofar as an original could be found. The charac-teristic of books copied by hand is that each one is unique: every man-uscript contains formulations, and often whole passages, that do not occur in other manuscripts, not counting the copyist's errors, spelling mistakes, experiments and clever ideas. What is more, few texts by non-Christian classical authors were passed down: by Plato, for example, there was only the dialogue Timaeus. Medieval commentaries on Plato therefore actually concerned the writings of commentators on Plato, the so-called Neo-Platonists, who themselves had not read the old sage literally but spiritually, and thus wrote about what had been revealed to them about his actual intentions.

One of the shocks that led to the Renaissance in Italy was the new availability of reliable versions of classical authors' works. When in the thirteenth century a Latin translation of the Arabic version of Aristotle's original Greek works fell into the hands of St. Thomas Aquinas, who was the greatest scholar in Christendom, it quickly led to an almost natural-scientific view of the world. Aquinas managed to reconcile his empirical worldview with medieval thought by proposing that the systematic study and rational analysis of natural phenomena were useful in demonstrating the truth of the revelations that people had acquired in the reading of the Scriptures. If the results of this study conflicted with those revelations, then the study was presumed to have it wrong. This was a great step forward compared with the lack of interest in, or even aversion to, reality that characterized most medieval thinking.

It was also Thomas of Aquinas who hit on the ultimate solution to the question of what exactly literal reading meant where the Bible was concerned. That the Scriptures were written by God meant nothing other than that the events chronicled in it were the work of His hand. According to Aquinas, the description of God's deeds was nevertheless the work of humans and thus open to critical examination. The literal meaning of biblical texts was the effect the writers of those texts had endeavored to achieve in their readers: the impression that God's truth was being revealed to them. In reading critically, the reader had to place the version of the Bible and the commentary on it in the context of the time when they were created, and to ask himself how that particular writer would have wanted to communicate something to his contemporaries – contemporaries who, like him, might have had very different preoccupations from the present-day reader. This implied a sort of division of the reader in three: the reader had to imagine the writer of the past and what he might have meant, but also the reader of the past, in whom the writer sought to achieve an effect; and third, one had to imagine oneself as a reader and determine what one thought of it oneself. This mental division of the reading authority is still the basis for the interpretation of texts.

In Aquinas' development of the idea of "literal reading," the written word was approached hypermedially for the first time since Antiquity, judged on its own merits and seen for what it was: a means of achieving effects. A reader no longer had to read between the lines to see the truth of the writing, but to read what was literally in those lines to find out how he might discover the truth of the writing. The visible, superficial meaning of a text was as important as any deeper meaning. This first step out of the Middle Ages was followed by many scholars, who began to read what the Bible really said, as if with new eyes. This led to a number of heterodox movements, which all referred to the literal meaning of Biblical texts, but were fought tooth and nail by the Church. And it ultimately led to the Reformation, in which the Protestant churches definitively broke with the one medieval Roman Catholic church. For Martin Luther, only the literal, superficial meaning of the Bible existed – to him, all esoteric knowledge that had ever been read in it was objectionable, attesting to human blindness, pride and arrogance. But then Luther was a person with a wholly "typographical" consciousness: to him, printing was "God's highest and most exceptional act of mercy," and between 1517 and 1520 alone 300,000 copies of his publications were sold. They were distributed mainly by peddlers, who reached every settlement on German soil.

Once people were accustomed to reading the Scriptures literally, they soon began applying the same method to "the Book of Nature." People began simply looking at what was there to see, without immediately trying to find a secret meaning behind it. This led to the scientific revolution, linked to names like Galileo, Copernicus, Boyle, Hooke, Descartes and Newton, which shaped the modern worldview over the course of two centuries. The writing style of the fathers of the natural sciences was even meant to be taken completely literally: the drier and duller the better. If a stylistic flourish did appear, for example a metaphor or simile, this was a shortcoming of the text, rather than the key to its hidden intention, as people might have thought in the previous thousand years. In scientific texts a distinction was henceforth made between descriptions of facts, which were essentially irrefutable, and explanations of those facts, which could be interpreted, discussed and theorized about.[24]

The newly acquired ability to simply look at what there was

to see also found expression in Dutch Golden Age realistic painting, which depicted the world as it showed itself to the eye, rather than filling it with traditional allegorical meanings, as medieval painting and the previous century's Italian painting had done. The realistic quality of the works of Ruysdael, Potgieter, Hals, Rembrandt, Van Goyen, Hobbema and the other famous names of the Dutch Golden Age does not lie in the fact that they depicted the world exactly as it was – for they did not – but in the strange fact that their works actually have no meaning in the classical sense of the word.[30] They refer to nothing other than the existing world. If you leave the Rijksmuseum in Amsterdam and walk along the city's canals, even today, you will see almost exactly what you have just seen in the old paintings. There was little interest in the work of Johannes Vermeer until late in the nineteenth century, because it was thought meaningless – until its brilliance was revealed by the arrival of photography, which also shows only what there is to see, without hinting as to its possible meaning. The work of the Dutch realists certainly can be interpreted allegorically – one can even read Amsterdam itself allegorically – but such interpretation does not lead to a better understanding of the work. That involves seeing the world as it is, and becoming filled with awe, gratitude and an occasional urge to laugh at the objective mystery of the existence of creation.

Before the invention of printing in 1440, renaissances of classical antiquity had already begun in a number of thirteenth- and fourteenth-century Italian city-states. The basis for the Reformation had been laid in the thirteenth century, and even as far back as the Middle Ages some modern natural science had been practiced amid all the astrology and alchemy. Such individual and collective achievements, however, could not be perpetuated, let alone disseminated, as long as there was no printing. The three great movements that led out of the Middle Ages and into the modern era shared a basis in refined reading and printing practices. For almost two thousand years, the writings of the Jewish prophets, the Christian apostles, the classical Greeks and Romans and their followers had been hand-transcribed by three groups: monks, scholars, and laypersons who worked for university libraries and sometimes monarchs' individual collections. Books had only existed since the end of antiquity, when the papyrus scroll was replaced by the "codex," a manuscript consisting of pages sewn together. The advantage of these so-called "volumens" was that they made looking things up in a text much easier: one could leaf through pages instead of moving down an entire scroll. At the same time, however, multiple texts were customarily bound together – but always in different combinations, depending on the available source texts and the interests of the book's owner. This meant archiving parchment and paper manuscript volumes was almost impossible. In addition, parchment was expensive and often reused (such manuscripts were called palimpsests): for example, a secular text might be scratched off and a Christian one written over it. Paper, which was cheaper, did not become available until the thirteenth century, when it was imported from China via Baghdad and imitated by the linen industry. Thus when an important "modern" manuscript was written in the Middle Ages, the first question was what remained of it after copying; and even if it was copied faithfully, a second question was whether a scholar would be able to find it in a particular volume in a library. Maps and illustrations were almost always made worse by copying and thus became less reliable; consequently, geographical knowledge hardly progressed for two thousand years.

All this changed with the birth of printing and the explosion of the book trade in Europe (in 1471 there were 14 printing houses scattered across Western and Central Europe; in 1480 there were more than 100, and in 1500 more than 225). Once a classical text was published in a run of a thousand copies, scholars in every country could compare the versions available in their libraries with the new printed one; this led to continually improved reissues in which the texts got closer and closer to the originals (which had been lost forever). With the development of literal reading, people had become interested in reproducing old texts word for word. Geographical and astronomical maps could now be reproduced with little loss of quality – first using woodcuts, and soon after using copper engravings, which allowed much greater detail. Maps were also updated by explorers. Slowly but surely, there arose a reliable picture of the world on paper, as is attested to by, for example, the many constantly improving reprints of Abraham Ortelius' sixteenth-century atlas. A similar progress can be seen in botanical reference works: after the reissue of classical texts, such as that by Dioscorides (first century A.D.), people began comparing those descriptions with what they saw in nature, and new flora soon began to appear. Plants were no longer valued for the moral and allegorical lessons they reminded people of, as they had been in the Middle Ages, but for their appearance and their medicinal properties. A new kind of researcher appeared: the traveling botanist. This led to such events as the discovery of the tulip in Turkey and its importation to the gardens of Western Europe – which, unlike medieval herb gardens, contained plants kept solely for their beauty (although these quickly acquired an economic aspect: tulip speculation). A comparable development can be seen in medical reference works: first came the purified classical texts, then revisions of these, and finally newly discovered knowledge with increasingly reliable illustrations. Printing not only improved the recording, distribution and archival of information, it also compelled the amassing of better information, and the new data in turn prompted the publication of new books, which in turn spurred further research, in a sociocultural feedback loop.[31]

Just as modern self-awareness resulted from the development, dissemination and internalization of writing – or, phrased differently, as written language called forth a "literate" environment in which the ideas of the self, the psyche, the ego, and autonomous consciousness arose seemingly automatically – the "typographical" environment of printed language called forth seemingly automatically the modern, scientific, Protestant Weltanschauung, with all its economic and political consequences, such as capitalism, democracy, nation-states and an international legal order. The fact that before goldsmith Johann Gutenberg invented printing in his workshop in Mainz, Germany, local renaissances, heterodox movements and scientific investigations were already taking place, and the fact that the invention of printing is attributed not just to him but also to others across Europe, suggests that around 1440 there was an urgent need for the invention of the medium of print. A social, economic and cultural breeding ground for a medium more modern than the copied book had arisen, and one was duly invented, just as before the discovery of photography a demand had arisen among the ascendent bourgeoisie for a cheap portrait medium to replace the expensive paintings commissioned by the aristocracy.[32]

Gutenberg's innovation was that he started setting type using individual letters and spaces instead of carving a whole page of text and illustrations into a block of wood, as had been done until 1440 for so-called block books. "Proto-typographic" block technology was extremely time-consuming and unmechanizable and yielded print of uneven quality. Gutenberg succeeded in printing books of uniform good quality in relatively high runs. He used a wooden platen press derived from the wine press and linen press (block books were not prints but rubbings made from ink-covered blocks. Gutenberg and his colleagues did not cut their letters from wood but made molds of existing written characters and poured in a mixture of lead and antimony to make the letter material. In its first fifty years – the "age of incunabula" – the new medium of printing remediated the old medium of the handwritten book, including typeface, text columns and hand-colored illuminated capitals. When the market for Latin texts died down around 1500, publishers had translations made in the various national languages for an increasingly book-hungry audience, and soon they were commissioning original works too. This would ultimately lead to the standardization of European languages, not only in spelling but also in the distinction between standard language and dialects. Bible translations, such as the Dutch Authorized Version, Martin Luther's High German version, and the English King James Bible, were an important early step in this purification processs. In the sixteenth century the printed book slowly but surely began to take on a form of its own, with title pages (useful in archiving), headings, page numbers and tables of contents (useful for looking things up in the book itself); with clearer typefaces and without ornamental capitals (which was cheaper); and with punctuation marks such as commas to facilitate reading. Every element of typography gradually became functional, designed to make books more efficient to use. Throughout the Middle Ages, reading aloud had been almost unavoidable, because the words were practically run together and readers could figure out what they were seeing only with the aid of mouths and ears. With the invention of printing, reading silently became generally possible and soon perfectly normal, and reading was thereby completely cut off from its oral origins. Printed language had even less in common with the spoken word than did written language. Acoustic space could now be fully displaced by visual space (although even centuries later there would still be remote corners in which unadulterated acoustic experiences could be had).

A page of a book is completely organized and uniform: it consists of right-angled columns of text composed of straight lines, and meant to be read neatly from upper left to lower right (Western writing). No one element stands out; only the empty lines catch the eye. The "typographic consciousness" formed by printing makes us inclined to (want to) see the whole world this way: in neat, uniform columns. Even the landscape loses its extraordinary places; all numen vanishes, even late popular forms such as gnomes, trolls and banshees.[33] Only what is visible exists. But the effect of a meaning apparently located somewhere behind a text occurs in print too – the difference is that for the typographic consciousness this meaning is not an ultimate truth revealed after long study, but a theory, an explanatory model. In this scientific approach to existence, the world is made up of everything that can be seen, plus the theory that puts it all into a context of cause and effect. Biological observations were only empty talk until Darwin's evolutionary theory placed them all into a meaningful, coherent whole. This is the power of a theory: it makes the world meaningful, whether or not it tells the truth. A theory is not an expression of an ultimate revelation, but a proposed explanation which is valid until it is refuted. Every theory can be discussed and criticized; in science, no absolute ideas, dogmas or laws exist, although some theories are more convincing and hardier than others. Theories are preferably written down in mathematical form, so as to eliminate the local influence of national languages. Galileo was the first to recognize this when he said that the book of nature was written in the language of mathematics.

To the naked eye, a forest consists of trees, plants and animals; regarded scientifically, it consists of an ecosystem of food chains and flows of energy and matter. The ecosystem is theory, the forest observation. In the typographic environment – the environment of the print medium – this is true for every phenomenon: behind every economic act and environment, one can assume there is a market mechanism; behind every social act, a sociological model; behind every creative act, a concept; behind every experience, a belief system. Essentially, nothing simply happens, even if the "simply" is all we can see on earth. In a printed text, only ink can be seen, but from it an experienced reader can draw the world of unspoken, unprinted intentions that makes reading such an exciting activity. What classical modern science, from Galileo Galilei to Isaac Newton, studied was not so much the visible world as the model or the meaning of it – that is, all physical processes minus their standard deviation. Only contemporary modern science has recognized that nature never does the same thing twice: everything always deviates a little bit from the ideal value that Newton recognized as the only truth. And only contemporary science dares to openly admit that it has no truths to offer, only probabilities.

It has even formulated the rule that every theory must be stated in such a manner that it can be refuted by facts: a statement that is always correct is meaningless. Such modesty and honesty are undoubtedly consequences of the fact that in the centuries since the propagation of printing, science has become the dominant worldview almost everywhere.

## Mothers of Romanticism

If writing causes the reader to realize that she is the one who determines the meaning of what is read (with the writer as the first reader of the text) – or, to put it another way, if writing awakens the realization in the reader that there is someone inside herself overseeing her own reading and interpretation – then printed texts take this abstraction process even further. The reader not only realizes that she is interpreting while reading and reading while interpreting, she can now also subject this interpretative process itself to interpretation. The printed word creates such distance from the text that the reader can reflect upon the manner in which she is reflecting. A writer must find a way to capture, with the help of words, sentence construction and a handful of punctuation marks, all the information that is transmitted non-verbally in speech. It is precisely this extramediality of written text, this loss of the meaning that goes unspoken but is conveyed through the voice, that makes it impossible for a reader to be entirely certain of a written sentence's meaning. Even a simple statement like "We will eat at eight tonight" is ambiguous without a context from which to infer whether it is an announcement, an order, a question, an observation, an ironic remark, or perhaps a hint at something which cannot politely be said out loud.

This uncertainty over the definitive meaning of a written sentence brings the reader first to the thought that she must interpret the sentence, and then to the insight that it is essentially impossible for her to be certain of whether her interpretation is correct. The extra step with a printed text – a third-order metalinguistic act – is that the reader realizes that every statement, even the most factually worded, is always ambiguous, although this is not usually stated. The written observation "There was a tree there" actually means "I am claiming that there was a tree there (but this text is not enough for you to verify it)." This raises the question of what the difference is between an announcement, a claim, a conjecture, a suggestion, an implication, a hypothesis, a deduction, a proposition, a thought spoken aloud, an idea, et cetera. From what does a statement derive its power? Is there something in the statement that commands authority? Does it lie in the writer's style? Or must an author first build up authority by means of extratextual activities – such as appearances in other media – before the reading audience is willing to take him or her seriously? Questions like these lead to the next thought: how is it possible that we understand what the text says? To ask this question is to answer it: it isn't possible. And thus the final thought is that every text contains a totally autonomous world which, to be sure, evokes emotional and cognitive effects in the readers, but has no ultimate meaning. Once one begins interpreting, all that is left is the "giddiness of interpretation" which ends in the conclusion that if texts are about nothing, it is because the so-called reality they purport to describe does not exist.[34] But how can this be?

The first people for whom the distancing process between meaning, text and reader led to the insight that written and printed text formed a world unto themselves, and thus should be treated as such, were the German romantic writers around 1800 (see box on page 130). "Alphabetization" had penetrated deep into these writers' psyches thanks to a new kind of language education introduced in German-speaking regions after 1780. Before then, the select few who were allowed to go to school learned to read through memorizing letters and words, without paying any attention to their meaning. The letters of the alphabet sound different rattled off as "A, B, C, D, E, F, G ..." than they do pronounced in words. A series of late-eighteenth-century writings about education attacked this abstract method of learning to read and replaced it with a new method based on the sound of words. From then on, pupils were taught to hear each word as a whole, instead of dividing it up into meaningless letters and syllables first and then reconstructing them through a double abstraction process into a meaningful linguistic unit. A central role in this Lautiermethode – "sound method" – was assigned to mothers: they read to their children, who thereby learned to hear words in their heads, in Mother's voice. Consequentially, for the first generations of boys who learned to read this way, the language had a huge emotional charge and impact. As they imitated Mother's voice, German (male) writers around 1800 easily achieved an

## 1798: Novalis on Absolute Language

There is really something very foolish about speaking and writing; proper conversation is merely a word game. One can only marvel at the ridiculous mistake that people make when they think that they speak for the sake of things. The particular quality of language, the fact that it is concerned only with itself, is known to no one. Language is such a marvelous and fruitful secret – because when someone speaks merely for the sake of speaking, he utters the most splendid, most original truths. But if he wants to speak about something definite, capricious language makes him say the most ridiculous and confused stuff. This is also the cause of the hatred that so many serious people feel toward language. They notice its mischief, but not the fact that the chattering they scorn is the infinitely serious aspect of language. If one could only make people understand that it is the same with language as with mathematical formulae. These constitute a world of their own. They play only with themselves, express nothing but their own marvelous nature, and just for this reason they are so expressive – just for this reason the strange play of relations between things is mirrored in them. Only through their freedom are they elements of nature and only in their free movements does the world soul manifest itself in them and make them a sensitive measure and ground plan of things. So it is too with language – on the one hand, anyone who is sensitive to its fingering, its rhythm, its musical spirit, who perceives within himself the delicate working of its inner nature, and moves his tongue or his hand accordingly, will be a prophet; on the other hand, anyone who knows how to write truths like these but does not have ear and sense enough for it will be outwitted by language and mocked by people as Cassandra was by the Trojans. Even if in saying this I believe I have described the essence and function of poetry in the clearest possible way, at the same time I know that no one can understand it, and I have said something quite foolish because I wanted to say it, and in this way no poetry comes about. What would it be like though if I had to speak? and this instinct of language to speak were the hallmark of what inspires language, of the efficacy of language within me? and were my will to want only everything that I was obliged to do, in the end could this be poetry without my knowledge or belief and could it make a secret of language understandable? and thus I would be a born writer, for a writer is surely only a language enthusiast?

Novalis, "Monologue," in: *Philosophical Writings,* translated by Margaret Mahony Stoljar, Albany 1997.

intimacy or Innerlichkeit in their poems and novels which is unequaled in world literature.[35]

What changed around 1800 was that written language went from being taught via a hypermedial route – placed as an obstacle between eye and idea – to being completely transparent, though what it made available was not so much a description of reality or an underlying conceptual richness but the emotional warmth of the mother's voice sounding out against the silence. This emotional charge gave the romantic poets hallucinations and deliriums in which all the fears and desires of their mother fixations were given voice: unrestrained by rational control, the language flowed from the fullness of the poets' hearts straight onto the paper. When the desires and fears centered on Mother were socially undesirable – for example, because of their erotic or sadomasochistic nature – then the writers found the most striking metaphors and disguises for them. These writers succeeded in saying things from and about the inner self that had never before been articulated. It would not be an exaggeration to say that they did not so much probe the unconscious as invent it. Before 1800 the unconscious did not exist in literature, music, or any other art form. After 1800 all cultural life is saturated with it, certainly in the German-speaking world. The unconscious is everything that has no outlet socially and yet must express itself. It is no accident that a century later, Sigmund Freud, who "discovered" the unconscious, observed that in the hidden layers of the (male) interior everything is about the forbidden desire to go to bed with one's mother and destroy one's father, the archrival.

Since romanticism the separation between meaning, text and reader has been a gendered one: the meaning was the son's love and fear of the mother, but the son could only survive the enormous suspense of the text he had written by making or keeping that emotional charge inaccessible to his conscious mind. Ever since, men have been writing without really reading what they have written. Women, on the other hand, did read, but did not write (with a few exceptions which confirm the rule). Language as it is experienced by men became detached from its content. At the same time as the early Romantics' *Sturm und Drang* appeared in Germany, so did the state bureaucrats, with their fanatical love of written instructions, orders, reports, forms, diplomas, memos and the rest of the mass of paperwork they thought were necessary for dealing with matters that could have been solved orally without much ado. The forms were filled up with hollow phrases by men who had learned to read from their mothers and then gone to the state school to be trained as public servants. In the evenings, they read the romantic literature that made up the lion's share of the publishing industry's product at the time – as opposed to the sober nonfiction, rationalistic essays and encyclopedic works that had been bestsellers in the previous century. As more and more began to seethe internally, external life became accordingly stricter and more formally organized.[36] The same was true for language: around 1800, the German in children's textbooks and all other official manifestations was cleansed of dialect, vernacular and animal sounds, just as students in the better schools were taught to speak without an accent. As a counterpart to the ecstatic language of literature, there arose a homogeneous, universal book-German, in which science and philosophy flourished.

There are two forms of writing culture. In the first variant, writing is a privilege of the elite, and thus a means of exercising power. Characteristic of this form is that reading and writing are not automatically linked. Just as there were many medieval copyists who had little or no understanding of what they were transcribing or writing in calligraphy, there were also many knights, kings, intellectuals and poets who could scarcely write and thus dictated their orders, letters, works and verses to read them over afterward: partial analphabetism. In the second form of writing culture, reading and writing are inextricably linked. Here, the social ideal is one of the "general education" of every citizen. In the German context around 1800, these two forms of writing culture converged: as a consequence of the roles assigned them in the general "alphabetization" of the population, men could write but not read, and women could read but not write. Women "do have taste, but not the creative power of a genius," as a pedagogical text of the time had it, with the consequence that until 1900 girls were excluded from the universities that educated the sons of the elite. Women were the subjects of men's poetry and belles lettres; in fact they effectively coincided with poetry in the masculine imagination – but they were not allowed to write poetry or have desires themselves.

Only after 1900 and the introduction of compulsory education did both sexes learn to read and write, though even at the beginning of the twentieth century there was great resistance to this: if workers and women were taught to write and do arithmetic, it could lead to revolution. Still, in the nineteenth century a considerable reading public had appeared, as the middle classes had received good language teaching. As a consequence, English literature, for example, flourished, the "high" as well as the "popular." It should be noted that this distinction is time-specific and somewhat arbitrary, for the popular culture of one period often becomes the high literature of fifty years later, just as many a lowly dish of one country is counted as haute cuisine in neighboring ones. In 1750 seven million people lived in Great Britain; in 1800 there were 11 million; in 1850, 21 million; and in 1900, 37 million. This population increase prompted a sweeping reform of the education system, which previously had been exclusively accessible to the elite but was now opened to all classes, leading to a robust growth in the publishing market. The most important popular reading matter after 1800 was the daily and Sunday papers, which were read in coffeehouses. Books had originally been very expensive – meaning libraries flourished – but the price dropped with the invention of the steam-powered printing press, and of rotary printing and paper rolls around 1810. The price plunged even more later with the introduction of cheaper papers, from alfa grass after 1860 and wood pulp after 1880, although cheap paperbacks were not introduced until 1930 and they only became successful in the 1950s. In the course of the nineteenth century, book distribution also improved greatly with the coming of the railways: kiosks and bookshops opened at stations to provide passengers with reading material, and these shops themselves were supplied by rail. In 1850, 2,600 books a year were published in Great Britain; in 1900 there were more than 6,000; and in 1912, over 12,000.[37]

In the same period, the reading public expanded from the elite to the middle classes and thereafter to laborers and farmers. This was paired with an increasingly far-reaching "purification" of English as a literary language. "Standard English" as we know it today arose in the course of the nineteenth century. This version of the language sprang from the dialect spoken in the East Midlands, which contains not only London, the capital, but also the university towns of Oxford and Cambridge. Everyone who was to take up a position in government or education studied in one of these three cities, where they learned to speak and write "pure" English. The students' speech was cleansed of local accents, and their writing purged of local word use and expressions. As more and more students returned to their places of origin after university, standard English spread across the country, so that all local versions of the language were suddenly downgraded to dialects. From then on, standard English was taught in schools all over the country, and everyone who did not master it could be unerringly recognized as belonging to the lower classes – and thousands of teachers and pupils from poor backgrounds became ashamed of the language their parents spoke. This development endures in our time: with pidgin English spoken around the world by people from different countries who need a common medium – not to mention on the Internet – the British still cannot resist correcting anyone who mispronounces a word.

To be sure, publishers all over Europe began to publish books in the national languages to enlarge their markets after 1500, yet until 1800 Latin was used as the lingua franca for education and scientific works. The pioneering philosophers of the Renaissance and the scientific revolution that followed – Descartes, Spinoza, Newton – also wrote in Latin. In the sixteenth and seventeenth centuries it was almost impossible to translate the content of subjects like physics, mathematics, medicine, law and theology: there were simply no words for a large part of the knowledge acquired and described in Latin. This was the same Latin that medieval scholars had written and taught in, and it was derived directly from the Latin used by orators in the predominantly oral Roman Empire. Latin was also full of the formulas and themes oral language makes use of to keep itself memorable, and a whole discipline had even arisen around the correct use of the language: rhetoric, or logic, which dated back to the Romans Cicero and Quintellianus. After 1500 extensive encyclopedic works full of expressions, sayings, pieces of wisdom and quotations were published for students and practitioners of scholarly Latin.

Until the nineteenth century, scholars and students were expected to write their poetry in Latin (with the occasional verse in Ancient Greek). Latin was not meant for expressing original statements – the point was that it be understandable to a male elite in the largest possible area and span of time. The goal of poetry was "what oft was thought, but ne'er so well expressed" – the best possible articulation of ancient ideas. A characteristic of boys' schools where education was conducted in Latin was their use of corporal punishment. When language education was taken over by mothers, and from then on conducted in the national tongue, for the first time poets' and philosophers' writing could be authentic, modern, and with the times. All knowledge was also gradually being made available in books, and the art of oral memory therefore lost its purpose. Intellectuals no longer had to exert themselves to preserve or retrieve already acquired knowledge; they could henceforth devote themselves to new knowledge and the unknown, and even admit out loud that they actually knew precious little, precisely because they had so much knowledge to fall back on. The romantic poets and thinkers could focus all their imagination on the strange, the faraway, the elusive, the inaccessible, the mysterious and the unknown. And if the marvelous world outside the well-trodden paths became too threatening, they could always revert to the known facts: they only had to pull the encyclopedic works off the shelf. The romantic preference for the strange springs from a great faith in the durability of the known. The same was true for the technical sciences of the time – romanticism coincided with the beginning of the Industrial Revolution. In the sphere of technology, too, people dared to radically change the existing world with the help of inventions and industry because they had gained access to a great wealth of durable long-standing knowledge.[38]

Poets in the rhetorical tradition, whose use of language and whole attitude to the written word are derived from the oral culture period, generally have a belligerent attitude toward their fellow poets. They want to be the best at articulating the (oral and rhetorical) knowledge which must be preserved to keep their culture alive. Competition is the order of the day – fierce polemics, making fun of other poets and exaggerating one's own achievements and successes – a way of producing poetry which is back in vogue among rappers today. Rap poets stand up and walk around, unlike their writer colleagues, who sit, even when reading their work before interested audiences. After 1800 it became possible for poets to be "creative," that is, to express new knowledge and experiences, perform new language acts. Since then, there has been no reason for writer-poets to challenge other poets. People can deem each other interesting or uninteresting, but they can no longer claim to be the best, for everyone is doing something different. The writer-poets no longer have to trouble themselves about being comprehensible to an audience, and in their poetry this translates into a concentration on image and metaphor· the "listeners" of old become "viewers." Because the poets also need not trouble themselves about what their colleagues are doing, written poetry is inclined to become hermetic, understood only by the poet him- or herself. The poet "lives only for himself, into the words," as a German lyrical poet expressed it. Romantic poetry and the modernist literature derived from it make up a parallel world alongside existing reality: literature as closed system. Voice became style. Orality was closed off via the mother's mouth.

# Typed Language

# The Return of Orality

From time immemorial, the sending of a message coincided with the recording of it on a carrier. Writing is the storing of language on a clay tablet, a pillar, a roll of parchment or a sheet of paper, with the goal of sending what is written through space and time. Printing standardized and made uniform this transfer. The first technical medium with which language could be transferred through space without being recorded it was invented in 1843: the telegraph. There had been unstable media for the transport of information before, but they had been biological in nature, from carrier pigeons to couriers who conveyed messages on foot or horseback from the center to the periphery and back. Tom-toms and fires were even earlier methods of transferring messages without a material carrier, but what was transmitted was not really language but prearranged messages (enemy approaching, the battle is won or lost, and so on). The optical telegraph of the end of the eighteenth century, which had a central post with movable arms attached that could represent letters, was so slow that only short commands or messages could be transmitted.

Texts in the true sense of the word could not be sent until Samuel Morse invented the electric telegraph, in which individual letters were converted into Morse code (short and long pulses), relayed through a cable and translated back into letters on the receiving end by someone who knew the code. An experienced telegraphist could decode about twenty words per minute. Derivative forms of the electric telegraph were the Marconi or radio telegraph, which sent a Morse signal via radio waves instead of electric cables, and the telex, whose transmitting and receiving equipment consisted of a typewriter-cum-printer and which required no specialized knowledge of the Morse alphabet. In all these machines language had to be dematerialized in order to be transmitted, and it was recorded on a carrier (a sheet of paper on which the message was written down) only at the beginning and end of the communication channel, although there were experienced telegraphists who could read and write directly in Morse code.

With Alexander Graham Bell's invention of the telephone in 1875, the stable beginning and ending state of the communication process also became a thing of the past: from then on, the voice itself could be dematerialized and transported via an electric wire. Early telephone users saw something spooky in the disconnection of voice and body, in hearing someone's voice without that person being physically present, and people thought they could hear secret messages in the static electricity noise in the wires.[39] This happens with every technical medium: after photography was invented, people believed they could photograph ghosts which appeared during seances, and to this day people report seeing extraterrestrial faces and secret messages in the snow on unused television channels.

In the case of the telephone, this submedial suspicion was partially awakened by the merciless character of the medium. The telephone is the first medium to completely fit the classic model of information transmission articulated by Claude Shannon, who not coincidentally was employed at Bell Telephone Laboratories, the firm that arose out of the activities of the inventor of telephony. Shannon's model described information exchange as a command structure, in which the receiver of a command had to signal back that he had understood it. When the telephone rings, it comes across as an order: one must answer. In the age of mobile telephony, indeed, it takes a lot of will not to. This command character of telephony, and the aversion of the person called to answer the command, can be heard in the word that opens a conversation: "Yes?" is a confirmation that a command has been received as well as an expression of doubt about the wish to obey it.[40] Printed language can only acquire a coercive character through style, in literary texts, or through the suspense of the storytelling, which dates back to the oral age, or, in non-literary texts, through the amazing or else commercially, politically or culturally attractive character of the information expressed. The telephone medium works with signals, signs that something must be done or felt; the medium of writing works with symbols, signs that something must be thought about, or imagined if need be.

Within a surprisingly short time, the electrification of language by the telegraph and the telephone created an environment which involved a new connection between public and private life in the societies in which it was introduced. The medial environment of the "global village," in which everyone talks to everyone else and is kept apprised of everyone else's business, began to come into being with the telegraph.[41] The first cable between America and Europe was laid beneath the Atlantic Ocean in 1858, and by 1861 all of America was cabled, especially along the railway lines: stationmasters became telegraph operators, as many a western reminds us. Daily newspapers in the US felt obliged to respond to the new speed of newsgathering and dissemination, and to that end, four years after Morse laid the first telegraph cable in 1844 between New York and Baltimore, they founded the Associated Press, an agency that independently gathered news and sold it to its members and vice versa. This way of working was imitated around the world. The hallmark of electric news is not just the greater speed with which it reaches the public, but also the strong reactions it evokes: if until then the average person had only poked his or her nose into the business of immediate neighbors and fellow townspeople, now he or she could become intimately involved with people all over the world. Reporters adapted newsgathering to this situation and began supplying "human interest" stories.

The Crimean War of 1854–1856 was reported by the English journalist William Howard Russell, who sometimes telegraphed daily eyewitness accounts of the wartime activities to *The Times'* main office in London. The English and Russian armies' inefficiency and bloodiness were no worse than usual, but because the English public was now being kept informed, as it were, "live," the senseless losses and all the human and animal suffering caused a great public outcry. This spurred the government to reorganize the army as well as the care of the sick in the British Empire, and made the nurse Florence Nightingale world-famous. Every new medium that supports newsgathering causes a greater public involvement in events elsewhere than before, which sometimes leads to collections of donations and political reforms, and at other times to indifference and cynicism, but always to higher sales and viewer ratings. At any rate, neither the telegraph nor the telephone became the globe-spanning media people take them for in the Western world: even now, in the age of mobile telephony, two-thirds of humanity have never had a phone conversation. One-third do not even have electricity.

The telephone is the first great delocalizing medium. If books in the national languages promoted nationalism and love for one's native soil, the telephone rendered space between conversational partners superfluous.[42] A telephone does not so much put speakers in two places at the same time, but in an abstract region which is separate from Newtonian absolute space. The proximity ostensibly created by the telephone springs not so much from the high sound quality of the connection as from the fact that on the one hand it removes all visual information from the exchange, but on the other it transmits nonverbal meaning-givers like tone of voice, emphasis, sighs and other evocative sounds. Purely auditory communication has a great intimate charge, which can make lovers of people who do not feel in any way physically attracted to each other (obscene callers and sex lines enthusiastically take advantage of this). Telephonic intimacy need not be erotically charged per se: more mobile telephones are used in China than anywhere else in the world largely because of the mass migration from the countryside to the city by only children, who wish to stay in constant contact with their parents, partly because they have so little immediate family now that each couple is allowed just one child.[43]

The involvement and physical presence evoked by the telephone recalls "mimesis," the audience's identification response to storytelling in oral cultures. The telephone is thus also seen as the first step toward a "second" or "secondary orality," a return to prehistoric circumstances via technical means, precisely at the moment when orality seemed to have been supplanted forever by advancing alphabetization.[44] After writing finally curbed the seductive power of the voice, it was suddenly brought back into play by the telephone, and later radio, but also by phonograph records, sound films and television. Secondary orality is distinguished from the preceding phase of literacy by the greater community awareness of those who have access to telephone, radio and television. Whereas literate people experience themselves primarily as individuals, oral people experience themselves as part of a larger group: the tribe, in the case of primary oral cultures; the group with the same lifestyle, in the case of secondary ones – a lifestyle called into being by radio, with its continuous music and its DJs (youth culture). In secondary oral cultures, the group can in theory be the entire global population, as with worldwide radio and TV broadcasts of the 1968 moon landing, the Olympic Games and other global sporting events, disasters and wars, and so on. The rich Westerner's sense of being responsible for all the misery in the Third World, however place-dependent, is one of the manifestations of secondary orality. In a secondary oral culture every person experiences him- or herself in two forms: as an intelligent and purposeful individual and as part of a passive crowd. The first form comprises part of the literary tradition; the second is part of secondary oral culture. The intelligent individual in us condemns and despises the stupid crowd member in us, while at the same time, as a sympathetic member of the crowd, we are indifferent to the solitary desires and problems of the purposeful individual we also are.[45]

There is a fundamental difference between primary and secondary orality. None of the technical media of secondary orality have a link to the body – precisely the link from which all earlier, traditional media derived their existence. Writing comes straight from the human hand, just like painting: the body of the creator leaves its traces behind. Theoretically, the identity of the creator can be read in every stroke in a painting, just as handwriting and signatures are considered characteristics of unique individuals, even in a legal sense. It is true that printing created distance between the body of the writer and that of the reader, but a book is still a physical object which the reader can touch, describe, sniff and crack: the reader's body leaves its traces behind. In spite of everything, the message still has a certain materiality.

In telephone conversations, the voice is detached from the body, travels, and reaches a body somewhere else practically immediately. The telephone is a material thing, a technical object which is held in the hand or worn on the ear, and in this sense it has a corporeal aspect. But the telephone always remains the same; it does not change with every message sent. The medium of the book, on the other hand, does: of each book, only the printed text can be transmitted (this changes with the "e-book," in which hundreds of books can be stored at the same time). The technical medium of photography is also bodiless – in a photograph, it is true, people can be seen, and one can read from the framing and perspective that a person has "sampled" the image from the world, but no body is present in the photographic materials themselves, for these consist of paper and light-sensitive chemicals which, so to speak, have not been moved in the making of the photograph, unlike the pigment in a painting. Photographic materials contain no photographer's "handwriting" to discover (though the message "behind" the photograph does: the style of depiction, angle, spatial construction, and so on). And something similar is true for the medium of film, although here the image becomes even more bodiless, being made of light projected onto a screen. But precisely because the technical media have no link to the body, they attempt to forge one with every means at their disposal. Photographs and films are made to move us, shock us, astonish us, provoke us, catch our interest, repel us: call forth physical reactions and become "real." Every technical medium addresses the part of the user's body that the medium itself has amputated from communication; and the telephone, radio, phonograph, photograph and film scrap the entire body. (See box on opposite page.)

Whereas in primary orality speakers communicate with the whole body, including the sphere of influence around it, contact in secondary orality is forged through word and image, not the body. Secondary orality is incorporeal, and calling it orality therefore is somewhat mystifying. On the other hand, radio and the telephone do cause us to reenter acoustic space. All sorts of phenomena familiar from primary acoustic space – myths, gods, primitive art forms – crop up again in the technical context of secondary acoustic space. Starting at the end of the nineteenth century, anthropological research into mythical figures, and the artistic reuse of them, exploded. In technologically realized acoustic space, humans are again connected to their entire environment, out of which every piece of information is coming at them simultaneously (via telephone, phonograph, radio, sound film, television and computer networks). The human organ the electric media help to extend is the entire nervous system. Electric wires extend the nerve cells until they span the world, able to hear and see everywhere – literally, now that a satellite network encircles the earth.

Whereas visual media like writing and printing keep the world manageable by dividing it up into fragments and specialties, sound media like radio and the telephone make the world a totality again, one audible whole, something a poet christened "the space of full life."[46] The telephone and radio make fantasies of conquest and empire into realizable plans – Hitler would have been inconceivable without radio, just as World Wars I and II would have been unthinkable without the telephone and radio telegraph. Because radio broadcasts from a single point, the medium is susceptible to appropriation by those seeking power, and its propaganda value thus proved enormous – until television appeared and, as a cold medium, made fools of all hot personalities. "Had TV occurred on a large scale during Hitler's reign he would have vanished quickly. Had TV come first, there would have been no Hitler at all." Every writer in the first half of the twentieth century who wished to give his or her voice a broader reach than was possible through the roundabout method of writing attempted to somehow get access to the airwaves – even if this meant supporting totalitarian regimes that opposed everything the speaker in question stood for.[47]

## 1920: Radio Killed the Vaudeville

Everybody believes it was the movies that killed vaudeville. That's not true. Movies, vaudeville, burlesque, the local stock companies – all survived together.

Then radio came in. *For the first time people didn't have to leave their homes to be entertained. The performers came into their house.* Gracie and I knew that vaudeville was finished when theaters began advertising that their shows would be halted for 15 minutes so that the audience could listen to "Amos & Andy." And when the "Amos & Andy" program came on, the vaudeville would stop, they would bring a radio on stage, and the audience would sit there watching radio.

It's impossible to explain the impact that radio had on the world to anyone who didn't live through that time. *Before radio, people had to wait for the newspaper to learn what was happening in the world. Before radio, the only way to see a performer was to see a performer.* And maybe most important, before radio there was no such thing as a commercial.

*Radio made everybody who owned one a theater manager. They could listen to whatever they wanted to.* For a lot of performers, the beginning of radio meant the end of their careers. A lot of acts couldn't make the transition. Powers' Elephants, mimes, acrobats, seals, strippers, what could they do on the radio? What was the announcer going to say, the mime is now pretending to be trapped in a box? The seal caught the fish? You should see this girl without her fan? Gracie and I had the perfect act for radio – we talked.

From: George Burns, *Gracie: A Love Story,* New York 1988.

At the same time, telephone and radio also make possible a more decentralized administration of worldly doings. The residents of new acoustic space begin automatically to search for spontaneously arising patterns in the audible world, rather than imposing frameworks or hierarchies on it, as writing required. History lost some of its explanatory power in the radio and television age; explanations for phenomena were sought in the present, in the connections, relationships and patterns that could be discovered now. This state of affairs is described as "post-history" – the counterpart to prehistory.[48] Radio, which allows the air to be filled with waves that can be picked up everywhere and made to make sounds, is a contemporary form of numen, the divine force that permeated everything in prehistory. The patterns that arise out of the world-as-ether are contemporary manifestations of the special and general gods discovered in the first acoustic space: junctions in a network of connections that an individual or community regards as vitally important; intensities of experience at moments when media make contact with the body (an individual's or a crowd's) from several sides at once. Whereas writing and printing tend to form closed, parallel worlds by detaching from reality, the telephone, radio, television and Internet conversely forge a connection with the outside, with shared reality. These technical media are, by their openness, preeminently unartistic in the modern sense of the word: autonomous art cannot be made with them. They demand, in other words, a reconsideration of the modernist (literate) understanding of art.

The phonograph was the first technical medium that allowed direct and continuous recording of the voice, without beating about the bush via written language or requiring fragmentation of speech into words and letters. The same was true of music, which until then could only be recorded discontinuously, by means of notation, but could now suddenly be continuously recorded on a carrier from a single performance and replayed an infinite number of times. This transparency of the medium had, and has, an enthralling effect. The continuity of the phonograph is greater than that of film: moving pictures consist of still images shown in rapid succession that are not recognized as such because of the slowness of the eye. But the sound on an (analog) LP is genuinely continuous – a miraculous step in the history of the human voice.[49] Yet something can be done to a recorded voice which is impossible in everyday life: it can be slowed down and speeded up, and even played backward through manipulation of the record (and later, its successor, the tape). This "time axis manipulation" makes the drawback of the durability of stable carriers even more clear: stable media are less reliable when it comes to the authenticity of the recorded material. This suspect aspect becomes even greater with reel-to-reel and cassette recorders, since messages recorded on tape are easier to cut up and rearrange: statements can easily be taken out of context, sentences separated by minutes of explanation can be spliced together so that they take on an entirely new meaning, and so on. Editable film has the same problem compared with live television (whose images could not be manipulated until the appearance of real-time digital technology). The down side of the credible unstable media is that their message is stored in the users' shaky memories, and thus quickly loses its reliability. This is why sounds and images are repeated so often on radio and television – the replay is a mnemonic technology. In the twentieth century, thanks to the phonograph, and to radio, which played the records over and over, music became the main memory aid for emotional states, at both the individual level (songs linked to certain periods in one's life) and the collective one (generations distinguish themselves from each other by the music that moves them). When one rereads a book twenty years later, it can turn out to be fluff even though the first time one read it one believed it captured one's innermost feelings, but beloved music continues to stimulate, refine and broaden the same spectrum of emotions as much as it always did, even years later, when one realizes one's past reactions to it were sentimental.

## Electronic Times

The mechanization of writing took place contemporaneously with the electrification of speech. The typewriter brought printing out of the workshop and into the office and the study – or at least the impersonal character of the printed word. Books about the typewriter seem at present to describe a distant past, even though the golden age of the typewriter ended less than twenty years ago with the introduction of the word processor. The typewriter became a transitional form between handwritten text and computer, but during the period when this machine was sweeping the business and literary worlds, it brought about a true revolution, if not in writing then in the gender of writers.

From the first demonstration of a Remington typewriter in 1872 by the daughter of its builder, Christopher Sholes, the typewriter was operated primarily by (young) women. With the typewriter, women made their entry into the office, and there they created a completely different environment, one in which opportunities arose for them to make the careers that had until then been denied them. (Another possibility for paid work was offered a little later by the telephone: until the late twentieth century, hundreds of thousands of women around the world worked as switchboard operators, putting through calls from sender to receiver.)

Until 1880, men were the sole occupants of the offices in which trade was conducted, industries were run and politics was discussed. They kept their hats on indoors, spat into cuspidors or onto the rug, kept the windows closed, chain-smoked cigars and left documents, magazines, ashtrays and other clutter lying all over their desks. The roll-top desk was designed so that the desktop could be hidden from view with one movement by means of pulling down a shutter. Offices had no carpets, wallpaper, or paintings on the walls; they were nothing but bare boards nailed together. Managers hand-wrote all correspondence on paper with ink, or dictated letters to secretaries, who jotted them down in shorthand and then wrote them out. Before they were put into envelopes and mailed, copies were made by pressing the pages with a wet felt cloth and then pressing the damp letter onto a page in a copy book, which was fatal for the legibility of the original.[50]

The arrival of women in the office led to a big clean-up. The typist transplanted the ideal of the neat, pleasant middle-class home into business culture. Lunch was introduced into the working day. Office fashion for young women appeared. Typewriter makers quickly realized who it was that actually decided which brand and model a company would purchase, and therefore not only aimed their advertising campaigns at the typist but also adapted their machines' appearance to her taste. At the same time, more and more managers bought typewriters to replace male secretaries and copyists, knowing they would get women to go with them. Special training courses for typists and secretaries were established, and millions of girls and women enrolled. A number of typists quickly ascended to positions as secretaries and executive secretaries. With the typewriter, women's liberation began via the back door, so to speak, for as the suffragettes of the first wave of feminism were demonstrating on the street for equal rights, the girls in the office were, with little fanfare, steadily capturing more jobs and social standing. Because women, through their typing skills, henceforth had control of the writing process, more and more writers became interested in typists – a striking number of male twentieth-century authors even had affairs with, or married, women because they could type. The typewriter was a machine for writing, so what could have been more natural than for a writer to look for a woman who had command of the medium? But this also introduced a question of power into the love relationship, that of who controlled the medium of writing: she who typed and inspired him to write, or he who wrote and kept her typing? Many a literary woman lost her life over this.[51]

Writing on the typewriter was discontinuous because the metal characters were connected by bars to keys that bore letters in capital and lower case. These keys were pressed one by one, the character on the bar hit an inked ribbon, and the letter appeared on the sheet of paper that had been fed into the paper roller. The letters were joined into words that were separated by means of a space bar. In handwriting, one places words rather than letters on paper, and the contours of a word are enough to indicate what it is. Because in typed texts every letter is equally easy to see, the typewriter compelled people to spell correctly. It was even used to teach children the alphabet. The typewriter keyboard also proved to have another use: it offered an unprecedented opportunity in the coding of texts for cryptographic purposes. On the Enigma machine, the German army's World War II encoding apparatus, three adjustable cogwheels ("scramblers") placed between the keyboard and the ultimate characters selected and printed a different letter of the alphabet for every key pressed. Because the cogwheels made millions of possible combinations of the same 26 letters, it was theoretically impossible for the enemy to figure out which code to use to translate intercepted radio messages back into comprehensible text.[52] This prompted the Allies to develop and build a computer in Bletchley Park under the leadership of Alan Turing, a mathematician who in a 1937 article had theorized that it was possible to build a binary, that is, digital, machine that could perform any mathematical calculation.[53] Turing called the apparatus the "universal machine"; at that time, "computers" were still people who performed calculations by hand, for example at weather stations. Turing would never have gotten the chance to build his theoretically simple but in practice highly complex computer if the enemy had not rebuilt the typewriter into a cryptographic machine. In Turing's machine, dubbed "the Colossus," numbers were for the first time used to actively do something rather than just to indicate a quantity or amount: the figures themselves were active.

The typewriter became a regular component of the computer in the late 1940s, when John von Neuman designed his "Von Neuman architecture" for computers, in which data were imported into the central processing unit (CPU) as input with the help of the QWERTY keyboard, directly borrowed from the typewriter, and the CPU's computing output appeared via a screen and printer. In alphabetic writing on a computer, what is written is first temporarily captured in working memory (which disappears as soon as the computer is switched off) and then, after a special instruction or automatically every few minutes, securely stored on a floppy or hard disk. On a computer, then, writing corresponds to saving step-by-step. As long as a text remains in the unstable working memory, it is highly flexible: words and text blocks can be moved and deleted without any traces being left behind in the text, as they would be on paper in a typewriter. Early computer users soon found it inconceivable that for centuries people had written with indelible ink. As long as nothing is printed, words in a computer retain a provisionality. Everything can be changed right up until the end, and there is actually no reason ever to end the writing process, other than the practical need for a writer to occasionally present results in the form of a finished product.

It quickly became apparent that the computer could be more for writers than just an improved typewriter. Just as digits in programming code no longer represent something but *do* something, words in computer texts can do more than just suggest meaning: they can be "linked" with texts behind them. One can click on a certain word (usually marked) and see another text. The second text is connected to the first not only operationally but also semantically: the reader's interpretation is determined by what comes before and after it. The main difference with pages of a book, however, is that a page of hypertext can continue on dozens of different pages instead of on a single succeeding page. The "hypertext," that is, the linked text, is non-linearly structured. Bearing in mind that until the early 1990s the average computer could display little or nothing in the way of images or non-text media, one can imagine how excited the first generation of writers were when they realized that technology had broken through the constraints of the linear form which literature had struggled with since antiquity. They enthusiastically began writing literary hypertexts[54] and announcing that the novel had been written to death, and that in fact we had reached the end of the age of print.[55]

What is unique about hypertext is not just that the written text must be read and interpreted – a second-order metalinguistic act made possible by writing – and not just that one must understand that one's reading of a text is just an interpretation and that others can be just as correct – the third-order metalinguistic act furthered by the printing press. With hypertext, one can also perform a fourth-order metalinguistic act: the reading, understanding and interpretation of the structure of the text as a whole. Fourth-order reading means realizing that the parts of a text can appear in different orders, trying out various orders, and experiencing the text's order or "outline" as the level at which its meaning arises or can be found. In hypertexts the main point is not the writing of an original text – quotes by others are essentially enough – but the presentation of a meaningful structure of connections within the text. Inventive readers can also make these connections in places the author did not foresee, because for any interpretation of the outline an alternative can be found that is just as valid. Hypertext, as foreseen and realized by the pioneers of the 1980s, sought to do the linguistic equivalent of what DJs would do with music in the 1990s: combine and refashion the other's sounds into their own styles.

What the first generation of digital writers did not realize was that the digital revolution they preached would consign them, too, to history in no time. Just as photographers who buy digital cameras are soon confronted with the question of why they are still making stationary images when they could be making film, video or television, authors who specifically wish to write for the computer medium find themselves confronted with the question of why they are only using words when they could be incorporating still and moving images, sound, music, voices, databases, webcams, chatrooms, games, e-commerce and who knows what else in their hypertext structures. Why should a link have to lead to another text when it can jump to all sorts of non-linguistic media? Since the arrival of the World Wide Web in 1993, practically every computer user has grown used to clicking from Web page to Web page and coming across not just text but also image, video and sound all on the same page: Web pages are no longer just pages of text with or without illustrations, but collections of media. It has thus also become normal to jump around using links without bothering to ask which server one is accessing and where it is on the 'net, rather than sticking around at just one URL. Why, then, impose the restriction of distributing a hypertext as a digital "book" on floppy and CD-ROM, carriers on which one can at most click from text to image and sound?

The first generations of digital writers felt compelled to insert their original medium of writing into their work as one medium among many. Thus they no longer spoke of "hypertext" but preferred to talk about "technotext" or "cybertext": that is, texts that confront the reader with the fact that the medium one is using to read is a machine, a material carrier. Besides, why should you be the sole author of your text when your potential readers have means at their disposal to help you write it? How can one ever again say that a book is finished if that book has become an open system? Hypertexts, unlike books, are localized not in space but in time. They are processes, not products. What good to a writer is a book that will never be finished? Practically every writer of the generation that witnessed the introduction of the personal computer has answered these questions by returning to the manageable limitations of the printed book. In any case, they no longer link their existence as writers exclusively to the digital medium, not even in the form of e-books.[56] And yet those fourth-order metalinguistic acts, as made possible or in any case intensified by the computer as text medium, are real and, looking back to the traditional literary canon, have a real influence on our reading of the old masterpieces. A substantial number of them have been discovered to possess a hypertext structure and an open form. With those old books, too, the reader had to figure out why a work had the structure that it did – and thus realize that it might have been constructed differently. Additionally, some poets now offer their new works in book form as well as on CD-ROM, so that what the readers get is not a final product but a work in the process of creation – for example, the versions of a poem slowly dissolve into one another on the screen so that one cannot tell which is the definitive version: the definitive version in fact consists of all the versions together.[57] The new literary genres are probably the discussion list, in which participants converse about all sorts of things in e-mails sent to every subscribed member, and the weblog, a site usually consisting mostly of text where articles about current topics and readers' comments on them are collected and organized.[58]

In the first fifty years of its existence, the computer has grown into a medium that has incorporated the previously existing technical and traditional media. Every medium is now digitally remediated, not just film, tape, LPs and CDs but also newspapers and letters (on news sites and in e-mail). Even digital painting has become possible: photographs can now be constructed by choosing colors pixel by pixel, just as traditional painters made decisions regarding the position and color of every brushstroke. Textile patterns are designed on and woven by computers. Online "chat" is a phone conversation conducted in writing: just as on the phone, the text is not recorded but vanishes forever as soon as it runs off the top of the screen. The digital camera made analog photography into an act of nostalgia. The fusion of the PC, webcam and mobile telephone made anyone with a mobile into a TV station. The proposition that the electric and electronic media have ushered in not a secondary orality but a new acoustic space is supported all the more by the fact that, at least at present, all the computer's capabilities as a Web in- and output terminal are being transferred to the mobile telephone.

The most important new concept that has emerged in the past thirty years with the development of computer systems is the "network," or the "self-organizing system": the realization that everything is connected to everything else and is constantly communicating and exchanging according to patterns which remained invisible to the linear view of cause and effect promoted by writing and printing, since these patterns were non-linear, vague, or half-orderly and half-accidental. Chaos theory – the "third scientific revolution" – would be unthinkable without computers, for the strange meta-order in apparently irregular processes can be discovered only with the help of a formidable amount of calculation.[59] Once taken up into the environment of the computer network, the world itself turns out to possess a drive toward order and life which goes against every law of probability and exceeds every kind of order that people have heretofore delineated – whether in the form of scientific theories like those of Galileo, Newton and Darwin or in the form of political systems like communism and democracy. The individual, too, is a self-organizing system, part of a network that exceeds all the classic human limitations of nature and nurture. This does not make us "post-human," as has been claimed,[60] but differently human. The individual is a "distributed cognitive system" in which no one central authority runs the entire show. The self travels all over (across media, landscapes, other people, spheres of knowledge) and forms a system of knowledge and feeling that is constantly expanding, contracting, rearranging and widening again. We use one of the elements of this system, language, to give a name to the system that is us: "I." I can walk past the furthest galaxies photographed by the Hubble telescope, and in the depths of my consciousness I feel the roar of the Big Bang. We live outside ourselves as much as we live in ourselves. If the history of the spoken and written word teaches us anything, it is that a "human" is not an unequivocal, natural phenomenon, but a being that changes itself time after time, with the things from the world it attaches to itself and with the things from itself that it connects to the world. This is a history that will never end.

# Practical Media Theory

## Introduction

One of the paradoxes of media theory is that if this theory were true it would not be able to exist. Book after media theory book tells us that we humans naturally exhibit the behavior that is preprogrammed by our media, and that we do not realize that our behavior springs not from free will or a sense of social responsibility but from the media we use to try to give that will and responsibility a concrete form. "The medium is the message" also means that when we believe we are saying something intelligent, we are in fact doing nothing but asserting whatever the medium we are using to express ourselves tells us to, or allows us to understand, to the exclusion of everything that is impossible to perceive, capture or communicate with that medium.

In hindsight it really is somewhat curious that, for example, in the nineteenth century people believed photography represented reality, even though photographs were two-dimensional, still, black-and-white, and much smaller than the reality depicted in them. In the past this phenomenon has been explained as follows: we humans become so enchanted with every new means of creating new images of ourselves that we stare as lovingly at them as Narcissus did at his reflection in the water; the new medium sends us into a new kind of trance or intoxication. But if it were really true that we become so addicted to our media that we fail to see what they are doing to us and simply want more and more media, then it would be impossible for a media theory to exist that was able to explain that the media anesthetize us so much that we fail to see what they are doing to us, whereby we only want more and more et cetera.

Media theory itself is expressed through a medium, and why wouldn't language be just as numbing as photography, film, television, phonograph records, radio or computer games? If media theory genuinely has something sensible to say about the way we interact with the world, then stories about media users being blinded are not just incorrect but arrogant, for they imply that only media theorists are able to see something to which everyone else is blind, in fact cannot even have eyes for. Bold "technodeterminist" stories are best taken with a grain of salt. Instead, let us investigate what we can learn, given the insights of media theory, about the effects of media on us and our perception, our body awareness, our ideas about art, and our environment, and figure out how we can make use of these effects. In other words, let us investigate how we can get the media to use us to bring about that which we would most like to see happen.

# Situations and "The Media"

"The media" did not exist before the beginning of the 1980s. What did exist was the press on the one hand and public opinion on the other. The press encompassed all journalists, whether they wrote for daily or weekly papers, filmed footage for television or independent documentaries, or made recordings for radio. These reporters kept to a strict journalistic ethical code which said they should report current events as objectively as possible and influence those events as little as possible through their presence and reporting. Subjective interpretation and politically tinted opinions were reserved for editorial commentaries, opinion pages and current affairs programs. There, journalists themselves as well as people involved in current events could give their readings of those events. From this position, "opinion leaders" tried to influence public opinion, and this opinion – sometimes archaically designated "the voice of the people" – was the only entity not directly involved that was allowed to influence the events that made the news.

The contrast between objective newsgathering and subjective or ideologically tinted propaganda proved to be unsustainable in the 1980s. When the TV cameras were brought into parliament buildings, MPs began behaving differently. Instead of making dull speeches and impassioned arguments, they began to deliver performances. As in any performing art, these were evaluated on how they came across to the audience. The validity of the arguments was pushed further and further into the background. The journalists could only conclude that reporting was equivalent to exerting influence – in the same way that observation changes an observed particle's behavior in quantum mechanics. Ever since this discovery, whenever press conferences and other staged events are reproduced, images of the photographers, camerapersons and radio microphones involved in the reporting of the event are always shown. The press's image of its own product has become an integral part of the information presented. Journalism no longer considers itself a mirror of reality or the truth behind public opinion. News is a product which is manufactured, like any other, by means of a creative-industrial process. The value of the product depends on its speed, uniqueness and aesthetic qualities – in short, its topicality – and is proven by viewer ratings, or entertainment value. If an event is to appear in the media – to become infotainment – it must meet the criteria of topicality and entertainment.

This development led to a different way of dealing with the press among people who for one reason or another wanted to get into the news. The fact that it was the presence of journalists that made an incident into a media hype necessitated a heightened awareness of how the performance would come across among those who caused that incident, whether it was an official opening, a protest demonstration or a public appearance by a politician, artist or musician. For example, while it had previously been said that NGOs – known as "action groups" in the 1980s – should not use or provoke violence because it would turn public opinion against them, now the press and public opinion were experienced as a single block, known as "the media." If you wanted to get into the media, a little violence or other conspicuous behavior wasn't a bad idea at all. While in the past the media had been used as a mouthpiece or megaphone to communicate one's own small message to the masses, from now on the media themselves were the target at which actions were aimed, for the media and public opinion were indistinguishable.

"The media" is less and less a collection of machines and their operators – formerly known as journalists – and increasingly a mentality: namely, the realization that everything is recorded but only a few fragments will end up as items in news broadcasts, current affairs and entertainment shows, and magazines. To become an item, one must provide mediagenic images or provocative statements. It has also become commonplace for reporters to ask, "Can you sum up this issue (a newly published or award-winning novel, a fight between segments of the population in an urban neighborhood, an unhappy childhood) in one sentence?" The answer "No, it's too complicated" spells the end of the item. What was once seen as an independent press is now regarded by all sides in any social conflict as one of the weapons to use in fighting, discrediting, "criminalizing" or even "demonizing" (as it is called in newspeak) each other. One no longer fights for a good cause; one stages one's resistance so that the media will pay attention, not in order to stir the masses with their public opinion to resistance or revolution, but in order to have been in the media.[1]

This absolutization of the media in the 1980s led to a great media aversion in all those who remembered a time when journalists reported what happened rather than shaping "media events." Cultural critics rediscovered the old Situationist manifesto *The Society of the Spectacle*,[2] and observed with dismay that its prediction had come true: any event on earth would henceforth be found interesting only if it presented itself as a spectacle. In the original French, the word "spectacle" actually means nothing more than "show" or "something that is merely visible": spectacular television programs such as quiz shows or game shows with lavish sets and dozens of extras were not a cause for concern for the Situationists. What they worried about was their observation that all experiences involving the entire body, experiences in which one "lived directly" – such as parties, drinking sprees and wanderings – were increasingly being displaced by experiences reserved for the eye alone (display windows, advertising, photographs, films, television). Marshall McLuhan summed up this development at about the same time as the Situationists with the words "An eye for an ear."[3] Westerners were increasingly being driven out of acoustic space, and a more and more visually oriented culture was developing. The Situationists of the 1950s and 1960s invented methods of generating authentic, complete experiences that could not be represented in images. When these were successful, when they went according to plan and a series of crazy incidents ended in a general party feeling, then, they said, a "situation" had been created. The main methods for creating "situations" were "dérive" (wandering through unfamiliar cities to the point of exhaustion) and "détournement" (distorting texts and images to breathe new life into them).[4]

"Situations," it turned out, could be bigger than the first rather lonely generation of Situationists had experienced. Every generation since has witnessed moments when a demonstration, concert or protest action suddenly turned into a "situation" that later assumed legendary proportions. Examples are the May 1968 student protests in Paris that ended in rioting, the concert at Woodstock in 1969, the 1980 squatters' riots in Amsterdam, and the anti-globalization "Battle of Seattle" in December 1999. These events were reported in the media at length, but exactly what had happened to the participants who created these situations was something it was impossible for the media to grasp. For it could not be seen; it had to be experienced through participating oneself: the party (for this is how situations are experienced) was extramedial, fundamentally unimaginable. People who knew each other barely or not at all suddenly recognized each other as old friends and got together, instead of simply passing each other anonymously, as is usual in the city. They met and got down to work, with no need for lengthy discussions about the hows, whys and wherefores. Out of these situations or "happenings" were born social movements that combined "direct actions" (or in some cases, nothing more than illegal dance parties) with special behavioral codes, fashions and lifestyles. "The movement is the memory of the event."[1] Every social movement of the last twenty or thirty years found itself confronted with the question of how it could maintain the "real" or "directly experienced" communality of the original event once the media had discovered it and turned it into spectacle.[5]

Some individuals undergo an extramedial experience and are left with a great fury on their return to the everyday media order. They experience their transformation into information as an assault on their lives and feel the need to counterattack. Their "antimedia movement" lets fly at the media, though it wants nothing to do with powers that fight against the freedom of the press, the hand that pushes the camera away, the soldier who fires on the camera operator, and all the other emotional images that are all too eagerly shown because they prove that the media still deserve the support of democratic society. The antimedials see through the conspiracy behind this monstrous alliance and demand that democracy break its ties to the media. They contribute by literally cutting the connections, under the motto: "We will reach more people by isolating and attacking the media." The antimedia arsenal is extensive: short-circuiting telephone switchboards, taking satellites out of orbit, burning down cable boxes, sawing down electricity poles, evading TV and radio fees, sending fake press releases, getting journalists to show up for nothing, immobilizing communication networks, cutting cables, cleaving monitors in two, painting over security cameras, altering data, creating magnetic fields, spreading viruses and worms ... Through such actions, the antimedials try to create media-free spaces that will allow people to meet when they suddenly lose the picture and come to find out what's going on. In these "temporary autonomous zones," the extramedial party is kept going as long as the media are absent, and stops as soon as they appear, usually in the wake of law enforcement.[6]

A second group chooses to appropriate the media rather than attacking them. One can do this in one of two ways: either by becoming a journalist or documentary maker and selling one's own products to "the media" in general (known as "the mainstream media" in this context), or else by publishing exclusively in the underground media or screening at film nights for allies in the movement one considers oneself a part of. The first method is that of infiltration, also known as "the long march through the institutions"; the second is that of antipublicity. The goal of infiltration is to get subversive or simply "good" information to seep into the media amid the nonsense, sensation and flagrant lies otherwise found there. The goal of the 1968 generation of students who began the long march through the institutions was to get the universities to provide subversive and "good" education instead of the biased, elitist, capitalist, Eurocentric, masculine knowledge they had served up until then. In every generation, against all prevailing fashions, customs and existing structures, a few individuals and groups manage to create or free up room for information, knowledge and experiences that have previously been kept out. As a consequence, science and art as well as journalism continue to renew themselves within the old frameworks (no institution can do without infiltrators who bring in new blood). The flip side of the infiltration method, however, is that if the self-styled secret agents succeed, and years later assume the positions of editor-in-chief, museum director, party leader and vice-chancellor, they become the very leaders they once waged war against, with the next group of infiltrators busily sawing at the legs of their chairs. Many, however, get stuck halfway through the institutions and forget what exactly the point of it all was (idealism? rebellion? adolescent carry-on?).

The other method of media appropriation, antipublicity, also has its pros and cons. It's not so much that those who start their own magazines, publishing houses, TV and radio stations, ISPs and websites are running the risk of unwittingly doing the same thing they accuse the enemy of doing. Rather, they tend to end up in the sectarian, dogmatic and argumentative "I am always right" sphere, with fatal consequences in terms of audience interest, at whom media are basically always aimed. And sometimes, after years of hard work, one is forced to face the fact that being right and being acknowledged as right are two different things, and pays for this lack of response in the form of resentment, cynicism or suicide. Sometimes, antipublicity does prove successful, and one becomes as big a player in the media game as those one once waged battle against – but that had not been the idea. The original extramedial experience from which the strategies of infiltration and antipublicity spring refuses to be translated into any media format; information, on the other hand, is always only just information. Outsiders can hardly distinguish between good and bad data. Even distinguishing between information and advertising is troublesome. According to McLuhan, newspapers fill their editorial columns with bad news so as to make the "good news" found in the ads stand out better. The only way antipublicity can really distinguish itself from the mainstream media is through design. Only by looking so cheerless, bungling or vague that reaching an audience beyond the real diehards would be impossible can it avoid the risk of being taken over by big media in search of a wilder, newer look.

The third option is to make no attempt whatsoever to translate the original extramedial experience into a form that can be transmitted through media. Instead, one tries to distort the media, to turn them against themselves, so that a different but equally extramedial sphere of experience opens up. This time, the media are attacked not on the level of their content or form but on the level of their carriers, their structures, their material means. An example is the cut-up. Take a printed text, cut it into four strips, and rearrange them, or mix in strips from other texts. An utterly dead author will suddenly begin to speak living language: the tone of his style remains the same, but what he says is surprising now instead of stale. Take a tape with someone's voice on it – say, a politician's speech or a teacher's lecture. Cut the tape into inch-long pieces, mix them up, and splice them back together, and you will hear a clearly recognizable voice saying startling things. Suddenly the politician will be stating his hidden agenda out loud, or the teacher's secret message will come to light.[7] One can also get a computer to perform this kind of détournements using a scramble program, as in glitch music. The point is not to intuitively or subjectively arrange the texts and sounds oneself, but to get the medium to do it, a medium which doesn't care a toss about its own message. Put a laugh track behind a random sermon or a speech, and suddenly the speaker will appear to be talking nonsense. A variation on these techniques is "playback on location." Play back the amplified sounds of a car crash at an intersection, and within a short time cars will be smashing into each other. Play the sounds of a violent riot at a peaceful demonstration, and shop windows will be shattered and police cars turned upside down.[8]

The fourth and final option for people who have problems with the media is to make art. All art arises from extramedial experiences. These need not be collective (though they may): they can also be extremely individual. In practically every artist's life there occurs a phase in which the person hasn't the slightest idea what she is doing on earth, and even has the distinct impression that there is something wrong about events on earth – until the future artist finds the medium with which she can begin to work. The linkage of the extramedial experience to the correct medium also generates the feeling that what one is doing is worthwhile, however great one's doubts about one's achievements might otherwise be. An extramedial experience, or the experience of the extramedial, presents itself as a feeling about which one cannot say where it comes from or what one should do with it. Or perhaps it is more of an intensity of feeling: the kind of feeling is of no importance; what is is its inevitable, compelling character, which seems to strip one's life of all meaning and even demand that one give it a new meaning. This new meaning is not so much the subject matter of one's work, not even its "handwriting" or recognizable authenticity (although these are extremely important in realizing an oeuvre), but rather the degree to which one is compelled yet again to attempt to express that which remains inexpressible, inconceivable, ineffable, just out of hearing range. This degree of need, this passion, is what makes one painting or book or multimedia installation insufficient and drives the artist to create work after work.

The four aforementioned reactions to media by people who have had extramedial experiences also appear in art. Thus, there is first of all a group of artists who wish to do away with art, for instance by refusing to create it any longer,[9] or better yet, by getting art to destroy itself (within a period lasting anywhere from a few seconds to a maximum of twenty years (see box next page).[10] Such action art and self-destructive art can be aimed against the embedding or falsification of art in commerce or capitalism; against the existing political, military and economic systems bent on destroying the individual and the world; or, even more broadly, against objective and subjective reality as such. The extramedial experience that underlies this destructive concept of art is that of becoming overwhelmed by the consciousness of the absolute value of art (of making something out of nothing), of the absolute value of life on earth in an empty, dead universe, of the absolute value of consciousness, and of things like emotion in an emotionless, soulless cosmos – combined with an awareness of the equally absolute fragility, transience, and futility of those absolute values.

A second group, instead of attacking art or the art market, elects to change it from within. One tries to infiltrate galleries and

## From: MANIFESTO AUTO-DESTRUCTIVE ART

Auto-destructive art is art which contains within itself an agent which automatically leads to its destruction within a period of time not to exceed twenty years. Other forms of auto-destructive art involve manual manipulation. There are forms of auto-destructive art where the artist has a tight control over the nature and timing of the disintegrative process, and there are other forms where the artist's control is slight. Materials and techniques used in creating auto-destructive art include: Acid, Adhesives, Ballistics, Canvas, Clay, Combustion, Compression, Concrete, Corrosion, Cybernetics, Drop, Elasticity, Electricity, Electrolysis, Electronics, Explosives, Feed-back, Glass, Heat, Human Energy, Ice, Jet, Light, Load, Mass-production, Metal, Motion Picture, Natural Forces, Nuclear Energy, Paint, Paper, Photography, Plaster, Plastics, Pressure, Radiation, Sand, Solar Energy, Sound, Steam, Stress, Terra-cotta, Vibration, Water, Welding, Wire, Wood.

London, 10 March, 1960
G. Metzger

museums with one's work, assuming the audience that visits these spaces will discover for itself that something completely new, real and better is being exhibited here than in other places. According to this model, there is traditional bourgeois culture on the one hand, and on the other is the avant-garde which livens things up, or else the outsiders who unmask establishment art as hollow, self-congratulatory and meaningless. This opposition is about inside and outside, the old and the new. The new in art, however, is new only because of the established art that makes up the archive of the old, by comparison to which the new can be new. The cultural archive is housed in more or less closed institutions such as museums, galleries, libraries, universities, magazines and books; where all the works and expressions that were regarded in their day as new, original and authentic are preserved and documented. The reason these institutions are interested in the new is because "new" carries within it the promise of an infinite arsenal of unprecedented possibilities, in contrast to the archive itself, which is by its nature finite. A "new" work is admitted into the archive if it succeeds in placing insignificant or profane elements into a meaningful, sacred setting in such a manner that they come to symbolize everything that remains outside the archive – the infinite number of possibilities that are not yet elevated to the level of culture, but from which the archive draws in order to maintain its status as culture. The "new" is thus something which is worth nothing until it is elevated to the level of absolute value in the archive – an absolute value that consists of the potential infinitude to which the work refers.[11]

The infiltrators who seek to introduce extramedial value into the archive of the old-hat are received with open arms, provided they are capable of disavowing everything old in favor of something that had previously been regarded as worthless by art experts. This also explains the alienation and the feeling of failure among many beginning artists: one wishes to devote oneself entirely to something that is worth nothing. The artist creates value from nothing (every entrepreneur's dream). The counterculture sees through this economic mechanism and founds its own institutions – often nothing more than a squatted building or an attic room – to create "space of its own" for art forms that do not fit into the archive because they do not seek to be "absolute," or because the value of what they present is not entirely apparent to either the creators or the audience because of its experimental character. This is how new media institutes and artists' initiatives come about, places where art photography, experimental film, expanded cinema, video art, interactive installations, Net art and other forms are shown for the first time. The institutions of the counterculture are usually granted short but intense lives, though they sometimes continue to exist in all their chaotic and irregular form as long as the original members remain alive. Some finally become recognized as guardians of the archive, or a particular part of it, with all the attendant subsidies, sponsors and market-appropriate approach.

A fourth group, instead of addressing itself to the organizational sides of the practice of art, attacks the very carrier of that art, not in order to create new content for an old medium but in order to manipulate the medium and make it express something that exceeds all human insight and is in that sense extramedial. Thus we see painters crumpling, cutting up and pissing all over their canvases, photographers scratching their negatives and treating them with acid, filmmakers burning their films with projector lamps, sculptors allowing their sculptures of congealed fat or snow to melt, net artists making their websites, and visitors' computers, crash. The artist's book also belongs in this category.[12] All this is the opposite of self-destructive art, that is, self-creative art, the work making itself into art. Conceptual art is a consequence of this approach: it raises the question of what art's carrier is – the matter and energy with which it is made, or the concept, idea or thought that informs this matter and energy in such a way as to bring about art. If the concept is the carrier of art, then however perishable the material the work is made of, the work will continue to exist. The concept allows new manifestations of the work to be made again and again. The concept consists of words, and is in that sense imperishable, or else it is wordlessly divine and therefore timeless. Getting into the cultural archive is not only a question of power – who decides what is allowed in or kept out? – but also a medial question: how long will the carrier of the art exist? In other words, does the work count as a contribution to the preservation of the archive itself, or are you inviting in, along with the new work, the decline of your own institution? Conceptualism claims that the only art that will continue to exist is art whose idea is indestructible.

The fifth way to work with media while knowing that they can never express that which has led one to work with them – designated above as the making of art – this fifth possibility also occurs within the sphere of art. On the one hand, there is art that is only concerned with art, which investigates the four points described above, plays them out against itself, raises them for discussion, and whatever else it is called in the language of artists' writings and committee reports. Reflection on art-as-medium: this is the variant that concerns content. On the other hand, there is a technical variant, which allows the medium to make all the decisions and generates a kind of sovereign art which seeks only to let the medium (or media) do its thing, whether or not there is an audience that will be interested in it. The difference with Modernist art is that while it, like sovereign art, sought to discover and glorify what was characteristic and unique about a medium, it did this with the goal of teaching the audience to focus on the essence and ignore side issues such as decorations and illustrations. To this end, the very museums and galleries where Modernist art was displayed were stripped clean and painted white: the audience had to learn to check its own identities at the door and become mere "viewers," mere perceiving eyes (instead of bodies which have to contend with belches and farts during art appreciation).[13] Sovereign art recognizes no difference between main and side issues: all a medium's capabilities deserve our attention, including its silly and crazy sides.

In this context the term "sovereign art" sounds a bit heavy; let us instead speak of "sovereign media." These enigmatic phenomena include radio stations (usually pirates) that do not broadcast news or entertainment, but only cheerful or gloomy, churning, bubbling noise; unlinked and linkless websites that make no sense; newspaper articles without heads or tails; experimental films in which no consistency can be discerned even after repeated viewings; artistic, or often very bad, photos of God knows what, and God knows why anyone would want to see them; novels that eventually force even the most seasoned readers to throw in the towel; and suchlike. Sovereign media do not seek to inform, but to bring about a meaning-free high through connecting, folding together, deforming, reversing, intensifying and dimming media chunks – sound, image and text fragments that one steals and copies from various places in the cultural archive as well as the profane mediascape and employs for one's own purposes. Sovereign media are authorless, for the producers of the programs, videos, books, et cetera are themselves absorbed as media chunks into the medium's self-absorbed serenade to the world. Sovereign media "relieve all information of its burden of informing us about anything other than its own sublime functioning."[14] What characterizes sovereign media is not only their lack of interest in their audience, but the fact that they always go unnoticed. Where no information is disseminated, no information is received. And yet these media are broadcasting more than just chaos. There are patterns to be discovered, an order that remains outside the oppositions of public and private, sacred and profane, old and new, enduring and transitory, in a parallel universe whose signs in our universe are unintelligible but very much recognizable as signs. Maybe it is not that the sovereign media are intangible and meaningless, but that we, the audience, are living in the wrong world. Connected to sovereign media, after a while one begins to wonder if the earth isn't spinning in the wrong direction.

# Analog Bodies, Digital Consciousness

The appearance of "the media" coincided with the worldwide spread of computers and the simultaneous increase in digitalization of all still-functioning classical "analog" media. Analog media can be defined as all media that are not digital, and digital media are all media programmed using a basic code of zeros and ones. The distinction cannot be made much more precisely than that. The original difference was that information was processed and stored in physical form in analog media, and in mathematical form in digital media. Consequently, analog media work with continuous data, in which there can be an infinite number of values between any two values, while digital media work not continuously but "discretely," which means that there can be a finite number of values between two values. An analog photograph, for instance, theoretically contains an infinite number of points, while the number of pixels in a digital photograph is finite and can be exactly determined. An analog piano can make an infinite number of different sounds; a digital piano can make only as many sounds as its programming allows. In practice, however, the classical distinction between analog and digital has become meaningless: computers are now so fast and powerful that the number of pixels in a digital photograph has become many times greater than the number of grains in an analog photograph, and the piano's sounds can be sampled and reprocessed into new ones that cannot be coaxed from an old-fashioned grand. Nonetheless, analog and digital media create very different medial environments, very different normalities, and thus very different kinds of consciousness of the world and the self. This environment can be described surprisingly precisely at the individual level.

A hallmark of analog consciousness is that its carriers always seek to choose a position in a debate (regardless of its subject) and expect or demand that others do too. Carriers of digital consciousness, on the other hand, always try to get an overall view of the field of debate in order to determine which positions are possible and which are precluded. While analog consciousness seeks to determine whether a statement is true, a reason valid or a picture faithful, digital consciousness looks at the conditions under which a certain statement can or cannot be made, which arguments are considered valid and which invalid, and how or when a certain image can or cannot be regarded as consistent with reality.[15] Analog consciousness searches for a single place from which to perceive and experience a reality; digital consciousness seeks an overview of all the places that make up that reality. In other words, digital consciousness always seeks the program of a debate or a situation, or the algorithm of a process. The self is the core of analog consciousness, while digital consciousness experiences itself as a distributed cognitive network. Digital consciousness is fixed in all the machines, books, databases, archives, interiors, friends and acquaintances, courses of study, e-mail connections, cities, vacations and other things from which it derives its knowledge and through which it disseminates it. The self is one element in this network, but definitely not the principal one.

Analog consciousness regards this digital craving for the big picture as a lack of courage, a halfhearted wish to keep all possibilities open: digital consciousness stands for nothing. For its part, digital consciousness accuses analog thinking of glorifying its own limitations. Why would you have one opinion when you can have all opinions at your disposal? Analog consciousness's answer: because the world becomes real only through that choice – it becomes my world, rather than a place for which I bear no responsibility since everything might as well be different depending on how one looks at it. One test of both kinds of consciousness, or of both ways of experiencing the world-and-self, is the encounter with something utterly strange or inhuman, such as an incidence of light, a weather phenomenon, a strange people, an animal's gaze or a vegetative feeling. Analog consciousness can register the unknown only in a language comprehensible to it, but because of this, the truly alien remains invisible and inexpressible. The "other" arouses a longing for the familiar in analog consciousness. Digital consciousness, by contrast, asserts that it can take in things that fall outside the personal, even outside the human format. An encounter with the alien and unfamiliar can rewrite one's inner programming.[16] Thus one can become a cloud, animal or plant, or communicate with dolphins or space aliens. The result is that after reprogramming one is incomprehensible to the person one was before one got reprogrammed. The advantage is that one subsequently sees through the new and strange as well as the old and familiar. In the empire of the digital there is no longing. "My" world is not that interesting: the only emotions worth feeling are those evoked by a seduction that comes from outside and is capable of transforming "me" (and vice versa). For analog consciousness, the world truly exists; for digital consciousness, it is a space of possibility.

In the twentieth century analog consciousness took two new forms not seen in previous centuries. These can be characterized in terms of the nature-culture opposition on the one hand versus the nature-technology opposition on the other. The first form, "nature-culture-consciousness," is pervaded with the realization that what is valuable in the world is that which has not been made by human hands, but merely taken control of by humans. Nature is real; culture is fake – sometimes beautiful, often moving, but fake. "Nature-technology consciousness," by contrast, knows all too well that everything on earth has been touched, created and changed forever by humans, but is valuable and falls under our responsibility for precisely this reason. There is no longer any real difference between nature and culture, for all of nature has become part of culture, if only because what remains of so-called real nature has no reason to exist except for the fact that humans have not yet destroyed it. Nature is the part of culture one encounters in natural parks. As a conservationist put it, nature is wherever your mobile telephone doesn't work.

Characteristic of "nature-culture consciousness" is its historical way of thinking. An example can be found in evolutionary theory, according to which all living creatures on earth are connected by lines of development going back to the very first cell in the primordial soup some four billion years ago. The life we carry within ourselves is the same as the life that arose then. All of evolution has elapsed since then, without human intervention. Yet the extraordinary thing about people is that they can understand the evolutionary process, in contrast to all other living organisms. For "nature-technology consciousness," on the other hand, evolution is something people can intervene in using genetic techniques from breeding and cultivation to genetic manipulation and in vitro fertilization. But a process much harder for humans to get a grip on is the ecosphere as living system. All the organisms on earth are connected by means of an unimaginably complex network of food chains and other chains of influence that run through and between ecosystems and their lifeless environments. This influence happens now, in the present – the past can perhaps explain how the ecosphere came to be, but such knowledge is not of tremendous importance when one is seeking to understand how it works and how humans can keep it going. According to the technical conception of the earth as a living system, evolution is an accumulation of knowledge stored in genes and bodily forms, and what is of importance now is how all the ecosphere's cycles work: how do they interlock, where, and according to which models? Our future depends on asking this technical question.

Digital thinkers never speak of history as a principle that links everything to everything else and creates meaning, or of the present as a manifestation of a single system that differentiates everything. Digital consciousness focuses its "posthistoric" interest solely on what is to come. The past is nothing but a database full of information, for which historians provide the search engines. The future, by contrast, contains no information, only possibilities, and the present is the first step toward it. Every new digital technology is regarded as if it were science fiction: before a new gadget even goes on the market, users are discussing what it ought to be able to do, rather than what it actually can do. The consequence is that no new technology ever lives up to people's expectations. To prevent disappointment, we must look at new systems, programs and applications that put unwieldy technology or biotechnology at our disposal and ask what wonderful things they will deliver to us in 10, 20, 100 or 10,000 years. For digital thinkers, the present is only of use when one looks back on it from the distant future and figures out what must be done to bring about that future, with its livable environment, stable political system, sustainable economy, space for the arts, and other blessings difficult to realize at present. For digital consciousness, all organic and inorganic life forms are connected through the lines running to and from that future.

Analog and digital consciousness – as they will be called here for the sake of brevity – correspond with the environments of groups of related media. In the 1990s these groups of media were called, respectively, "old " and "new." The environment of a collection of media is probably better designated a "meta-environment," since it is located one level of abstraction above the environments or normalities that accompany specific media. McLuhan was already in the habit of lumping media together and describing their collective environments: when he spoke of "electricity" as an extension of the human nervous system, he was referring to the telephone, television, radio and all the electric and electronic media that can be used to gather information from the world and disseminate it, including computer networks, which did not yet really exist in his day but which he already envisioned (McLuhan, too, thought about technology as if it were science fiction).

In the metaclass of analog consciousness, we can distinguish many subclasses that are connected to specific analog media. Whether such distinctions can be made in digital consciousness is not yet clear.

Twentieth-century forms of analog consciousness are easy to tell apart in terms of the era's three dominant types of image (which are complemented by the three dominant types of sound). The three types of image are photography, film and video. The simplest descriptions of these media are as follows: a photograph is a still image, a film is an image that moves within its frame, and a video is an image that transforms within its frame. Similarly, the soundtracks of these media differ: photography is silent; cinematic sound creates the impression of being "natural" (even if it is often mixed from dozens of different sources); and video sound seems distorted, or at least unnatural. The latter is true even in music videos: when these contain naturalistic sounds, such as the noise of a streetcar seen on screen, they come across as special effects amid all the other sounds, which are unnatural because they have been composed. Three kinds of consciousness or mentality are linked to the three categories of stillness, movement and transformation; each manifests itself in a particular manner of dealing with one's physical existence, one's own body and the bodies of others. These bodily habits can be deduced from the respective technical qualities of photography, film and video, and they are separate from the cultures in which the bodies function and the people live. These three different ways of dealing with the body – these forms of body awareness or "consciousness" – determine in large part how people live in those cultures: in other words, which cultural elements they choose from in forming worldviews and life practices.[17] When people around the world began using the same media in the twentieth century, it became possible for them to understand and appreciate each other. The most popular photography exhibition and book of the twentieth century, *The Family of Man* (1955), showed the inhabitants of earth that human behavior, when captured by the camera, was the same everywhere.

A photograph shows a reality at rest. This reality need not do anything special: it simply is what it is. Even when a picture is of people self-consciously showing off, it depicts the showing off as a natural fact, something which is visible and thus possible to photograph. And thus a photograph of a spectacle or a high-speed event is not itself spectacular or fast, but as motionless and open to protracted inspection as a portrait of a handsome man. Photography represents the world as a natural fact, as something which exists and remains itself, a world which can be closely examined and accepted without reservation, however things might look in it and whatever social judgments there are about it. This fundamental capacity of photography can also be seen in one of the ways people have of dealing with their bodies: they accept them completely as they are, even when they are doing or achieving nothing. It is enough that they are themselves; this alone makes them worthy of our attention. The "photographic body" experiences and presents itself as a natural fact; we will therefore call it the "natural body." It can be characterized as follows.

The natural body knows it is natural, but becomes conscious of that naturalness only when it stops feeling natural, say, because of one too many cups of coffee, an allergic itch, a cut on the skin, an approaching period, a headache, jet lag, a giggle fit, infatuation, heavy manual labor, a drag on a joint, a beer, a moment of absent-mindedness, a vague physical malaise. The natural body has found the point at which it is what it is (and that's all it is). It has an essence, an inviolable core, a stable inner norm, but it only learns what this is by deviating from it. It is ashamed of this deviation: what characterizes the natural body is its capacity for shame. The natural body is relaxed about its health. The exercises it performs are intended to keep its muscles strong and thus increase its naturalness, not to make itself appear more beautiful than it really is. The natural body does not rely on external beauty or normality but on charm. Children with Down's Syndrome can have wonderfully natural bodies, as Diane Arbus has demonstrated in her photography. When the natural body dances, it does so around a stable point located somewhere in the torso, and it does not even need music, as performers of free dance like Isadora Duncan showed us at the beginning of the twentieth century: in her own words, she was acting "perfectly naturally."[18]

The natural body has a relaxed attitude toward technology: it does not find it threatening but useful, often enjoyable, and interesting. It likes to surround itself with man-made trinkets, the better to bring out its own naturalness. The only thing it is afraid of is the unnatural; it prefers to give this a wide berth rather than confronting it. When the natural body loses its fight against the unnatural, it becomes addicted. Addictions maintain bodies which cannot exist on their own. In photographs, bodies are always isolated in space: even when there is a crowd of people in the frame, each one can be looked at and recognized separately. Every natural body is an individual, and for the natural body everyone else is always an individual too. The natural body is not above participating in group behavior, even if it's just for fun, but in its heart it prefers to stand on its own two feet. For the natural body, solitude is the source of all art: photographers, authors and dancers work alone. To the natural body, the goal of life on earth is to become replaceable, for every body is part of a series of bodies which have been replacing each other for billions of years and will, with luck, continue to do so for billions of years more. In its own life, the natural body sometimes undergoes moments at which it seems to break out of this history. At these moments, ones of absolute stillness in space and time, it experiences the meaning of its existence and the infinite value of life. The natural body calls such instants "endless days" or "everlasting moments."

People are their bodies only to a certain degree. The something extra that does not coincide with one's physical being allows one to direct one's body. One does this on the basis of a self-image discovered in one's body. No one is or has a natural body, but a person can glorify the natural body and act accordingly because he thinks he has or is one. The self-image discovered in the body owes its existence to a medium. In this case, the medium is photography. A body with a cinematic self-image behaves and experiences itself very differently: it glorifies movement, not stillness. In a film, movement begins with the first image and goes on until the end. A film therefore moves in a direction, based on a script, written or unwritten, and there is a director or producer who determines this direction and keeps an eye on it, acting as a leader and as the one with the power. A film is never made by one person, but always by a group (besides the director, there is also a producer, a sound technician, an editor, actors, set designers, an art director and so on). Also, a film, unlike a photograph, is not seen by one person at a time but by a crowd of people in a cinema. Even when we see a film alone at a matinee, we experience the crowd around us in the form of the empty seats. After the film's closing image, the visitor undergoes a radical reversal in returning to everyday reality. We see all these features in the cinematic body, which we will call the "ideological body": that is, a body with an ideology, an intent to become something other than what it is.

Photography shows us what a body is; film shows us what it can become. The ideological body does not have a stable internal norm like the natural body; under its skin it experiences chaos, unrest and confusion, and its response is an aversion to this or an unhappy consciousness of it. Because of its dynamic disposition, however, the ideological body does not take this lying down but goes in search of a new norm, an external norm which it imposes upon itself from the outside – or, more often, allows to be imposed on itself. The ideological body seeks a director to design or guide the screenplay of its life story, a leader or a guiding principle. It also lays out – continuously and unsolicited – the abstract frameworks that form the basis of its behavior, and the moral implications of these rules. When the ideological body fails to live up to its external norm, it does not experience the misstep as a deviation it feels ashamed of, as the natural body does, but as a transgression it feels guilty about. The ideological body knows guilt rather than shame. Because of the danger of violating the norm, the ideological body tries to rely as little as possible on feeling, and to make "conscious" or "active choices" instead of reacting spontaneously. The ideological body is always busy proving that it is free and has a will of its own. It believes in heroic gestures, self-conquest, achievement. It must do something to feel that it has a right to exist. It does not accept the world as it is blindly and in advance. The ideological body is interested in world events, in the movement which brings everything together; it is prepared to listen to arguments and to reflect. It likes to sign up for courses. It takes the world seriously, as it means to be serious itself. To the ideological body, human beings are interesting objects of study.

The ideological body perceives technology as threatening. Before the machines take over, it wishes to make a gesture, a justified reaction, an assault on the inevitability of fate. The ideological body has lost faith in the resistance of the flesh, but that means it enjoys the dizziness of speed, the conquest of materiality, that much more. Addiction is the ideological body's natural state, and staying unspoiled requires active effort. The body helps keep a technical society running, but on the weekends it draws refreshment from nature, in the park or outside town, in sports and games, sun- and air-bathing, or by exercising, running, cycling or swimming in a group. The ideological body sees human beings as conquerors of nature – of nature's murky depths but also of the capacity to act naturally themselves in their spare time. It is animated not by a feeling of power or pride, but one of freedom: "You can't touch me." It is happy to be prescribed a norm, for norms cannot affect it. The outside world always remains outside: the ideological body internalizes nothing. It makes no difference which external order it joins, as long as movement is the result. This is why it can be fascist or communist for years and then suddenly become democratic. There is no ultimately stable state in the program of the ideological body.

Whereas natural bodies are unique and individual, ideological bodies have no special characteristics. They all look alike. The ideological body is representative: it stands for a thought, an expression of will. Therefore it does not matter who it is personally – it can be anyone. The ideological body is a true "mass man." It always wants to be part of a mass movement, in sports as well as politics, world history, and even the cosmos if all else fails. It strives for world power, to embrace all the world. If it achieves such power, it hopes to mutate into something completely different: a benefactor, a laborer, an Übermensch, a world citizen, a higher consciousness, a being from space. The ideology attached to the body offers an idea of the coming mutation. Everything must always have an identity, a function in the ideological system. Even when the ideological body dances, it doesn't do it for no reason, but for the good of its health: it performs rhythmic-hygienic movements, either to restore its past naturalness or to prepare itself for its future mutation. Just as a body in a film can perform various movements but never change into something totally different – since film must always remain realistic and naturalistic – the ideological body must always stay stuck in its old state. But this only makes the dream of the new more exciting: attractive but also frightening. The ideological body is bored; it cannot accept what it is, but it is unable to change, for all it can do is move, be dynamic, storm forward, or long for the good old days. The natural body, by contrast, never gets bored.

The video image, the third image type of the twentieth century, is unnaturalistic. It is always visibly manipulated, not only in the relationship between images (as in film, which is edited), but also within the image frame. With a video of a movie, one can pause and rewind, review fragments, and then continue playing the tape, or turn it off if it's no good. A film on videotape has lost its power over the audience, a power to which one must blindly surrender in the theater. The video image no longer exercises any force: it is controlled by the viewer. Film shows us a dynamic story which ends in a final insight, or at least a single closing image. Video does not follow a story line, but instead throws up a cloud of connections and relationships. Video strives not for realism or honesty but for compression. An editor can cut an entire feature film down to three minutes, as for a trailer or video clip; and thirty seconds of a news broadcast is sufficient to represent the day's most important event. A video image is constructed out of highly charged fragments. In video the picture and soundtrack roll independently of each other, giving each other double and ironic meanings and placing each other in a different, sharper light. Once the sound on a videotape is turned off, the noises in the room take over their role. Video no longer needs a world to depict: having photographic and cinematic images to transform is enough. The video image is invisible when the VCR is switched off, unlike the images in a film, which can always be seen whether or not the reel is running through the projector. Videotape is black.

The body with a video outlook, or a video self-image, is the "technical body." If the natural body glorifies stillness and the ideological body absolutizes movement, the technical body is in love with metamorphosis or transformation. The technical body is a piece of nature that has appropriated technology. If the natural body has a stable internal norm, and the ideological body follows an imposed external one for lack of inner stability, the technical body alters its internal norm and then realizes the new one with the genetic and social raw materials at its disposal. To change one's body's inner norm, one must first accept that body as it is and then, step by step, discover what it can do. Beginners can measure themselves against others all they like, but anyone who has ever worked out knows that no two bodies are or can be the same, even if they are subjected to the same training program. Permanent training is necessary, for left to itself a body will automatically sink back into its old state. The technical body knows no shame or guilt, but it is capable of shyness. It is able to feel uncomfortable. The technical body's new, self-designed norm is unstable, though no less convincing for that. The technical body is a body attached to machines.

The technical body knows about existing ideologies, but it is unimpressed by them. Racism – biological conceit – falls outside the technical body's sphere of understanding. Sex, technically speaking, is the transmission of a bodily fluid through a tube into a cavity. A leg press leads to big thighs, herbal tea to a good night's sleep; big people are more persuasive at selling athletic shoes. The technical body is interested in all methods: cultural, medical, esoteric. It experiments with them until it finds out which approach works best. The technical body knows how important it is. To it, everything current is worth the trouble. Plastic surgery, fitness – the smell of butyric acid in gyms – genetic scanning, hormone treatment, artificial insemination, in vitro fertilization, abortion clinics, the Pill, organ transplants, life extension, viral immunity enhancement, environmental monitoring, temperature regulation, computer networks, gigachips, telematics, satellites, space probes, extraterrestrial biology, artificial life: the technical body's program is big enough for a universe, but it runs on a single blue-and-white planet. The technical body is a world body. It does not strive for power, but for strength, compactness, a gathering together. At its moment of maximum concentration, it carries in itself all of humanity's gene pool, rolled up together into a single code. The young Schwarzenegger said, "Eventually, I wanted every single person who touched a weight to equate the feeling of the barbell with my name. The moment he got hold of it I wanted him to think: 'Arnold.'" For the technical body, the meaning of life is a quantitative issue: if one refrains from doing this or that, one simply accumulates a bit less meaning. It makes a difference whether you spend your vacation in the Himalayas or at a campground on the beach. The technical body knows a parallel universe of utmost concentration, where everything is endlessly transforming, outside space and time, life and death. As the natural body experiences an eternal instant and the ideological body anticipates a definitive mutation, the technical body discovers immortality, a program irrepressibly rewriting itself, a nanotechnology of consciousness.

In the twentieth century, a great many statements were made about subjects such as life, Being, the nature of reality, the existence of the world, religion, the origins of literature and other media, the meaning of music, and our responsibility for our fellow humans – to name a random selection of subjects about which a person can believe something. What such statements revealed was not so much the deeply human or personal experiences of whoever made them but his or her assimilation of the effects of a predominant twentieth-century medium. Why would one see one's life flash by like a movie just before dying? Why not as a photo album, or a video? Why not a radio program in which one heard all the important voices in one's life one last time? Every interpretation of anything is medially determined. This insight inspires modesty, but also a distrust of any statement that says anything definite about things we can never really know about. A life full of movement is not in itself more valuable, real or interesting than the life of someone who sits around doing nothing or whose personality continually changes. Conversely, it is true that to learn about movement we need the ideological body, need to learn to look with a cinematic eye. What the ideological body can tell us about stillness is not incorrect, but it is uninteresting: the ideological body experiences stillness as an absence of movement. For the natural body, however, stillness is the presence of something movement cannot touch: the immovable, which is "so full of itself." And those who would rather come to know metamorphosis from the inside out need the technical body.

This evokes the question of what the digital self-image might be. Anything digitally presented or represented can be brought to a stillstand, put into motion or transformed, down to the pixel level. When computers became able to digitally record and reproduce every image type, the three "bodies" described above began to merge. Just as any software program can theoretically run on any computer, any body program can run on any body. Digital consciousness can choose which body it wishes to be in which circumstances, down to its stupidest, most brilliant, most profound and most superficial traits. The body is as much a space of possibility as any other social domain or medial environment. Identity, as a way of being, a basis for existence and a framework for identification which one acquires once and for all, is something one can impose on oneself and others, but this is unnecessary. The digital body – to provisionally call it that – has an unstable identity; in fact, it is devoid of identity and therefore able to take on any identity without having to fear lasting consequences. Natural, ideological and technical bodies are options for a digital consciousness, but other forms of physical and mental existence are also imaginable and therefore realizable. For digital consciousness, nature and technology coincide: technology is a form of nature, and nature a form of technology. They are two methods of solving problems concerning physique and behavioral strategies, two methods of evoking and playing out desires, of giving in to temptations or resisting them. But there are also other methods. One is art.

# The Virtual Object of Interactive Art

At the introduction of any new medium, people immediately attempt to create new art with it. The questions that then arise are whether what has been made is art; if so, what about it makes it art; and if not, what is it? Works of art made with older media, owing to their long lives and the unceasing activity of critics, art historians and cultural philosophers, are framed within various contexts, discourses and networks that guarantee their status as art. Art is thus seen as an expression of its time and as an image of the zeitgeist. Or else it is seen as a carrier of aesthetic and spiritual values which transcend its time and thus remain captivating and relevant to later generations. Art is also seen as expressing insights about the general human condition or humanity's place in the cosmos – insights which have nothing to do with time because they touch on a timeless, eternal or immortal domain beyond the material world. Art is also the preferred means of attacking, repudiating and surpassing the age in which one lives, including its so-called eternal values. Art is used to attack the art market as a symbol of the capitalist establishment under which artists must sell their products. And so on. If one wishes to exhibit new media art as art, one can always find arguments in support of doing so. A characteristic of the preceding series of ideas about art, however, is that they are about not the works themselves but the social, economic, psychological and cultural role art can play. From the viewpoint of media theory these approaches are uninteresting, for the question media theory asks is what it is about a work that makes it artistic. How must one use a medium if one wishes to make something that can be called art? Which medial effects must be achieved in order for art to be produced? Once this is known, is becomes possible to say what is artistic about art made with the newest media, irrespective of context. This question will be answered below with respect to the interactive art that has been presented as such for the past twenty or so years.

A system is interactive if it is flexible enough to adapt to the way people use it, and if conversely the users are also altered by the changes they cause in the system. In other words, when two systems are linked together and through that linkage change each other, there is interactivity. If an animal changes its environment by digging holes and subsequently adapts its way of living to the shelter offered by those holes, for instance by keeping to routes through the landscape that lead directly to (or stay as far as possible from) the hole, and consequently form tracks in that landscape through which water drains away in the rainy season, taking twigs and loose earth with it and thus creating a niche for pionieer plants, which are visited by butterflies or bees which had previously not been drawn to that location, leading to the coming of caterpillar-eating titmice, which themselves become food for sparrow hawks and other small birds of prey, which in turn build holes and nests and in due course carry off the young of the animal that dug that first hole – we can sum up this long, gradual, complex process as inter-activity between animal and landscape.

This raises the question of whether every act is interactive, caused by something outside the actor and intervening in that external force as well as affecting the actor. The opposite, 'interpassivity', is only possible under extremely specific conditions.[20] One must have total control over one's environment to prevent anything in that environment from changing or causing changes to oneself. It takes a colossal effort to lie on the sofa night after night, year after year, watching television, chips and beer at hand, without becoming informed in any way by what one sees on the tube, nor exercise any influence at all on the various channels' programming. This colossal effort is focused first of all on the social context, which one must organize down to the details in order to meet the desired consumption level; second, on the person of the couch potato, who must be disciplined into non-reaction down to the slightest change in mood; and third, on the market researchers for the various TV channels, who must on no account be allowed to find out what their heaviest consumers find enjoyable, fascinating or irritating. One solution could be to record television programs and then tape them without watching them, just as one could refuse to read the books on one's shelves. Yet in both examples there is interactivity: the unwatched tapes and unread books contain potential future time, time one hopes to make someday to watch or read them. And so they do exercise influence on their owners, as possibilities, just as their owner can determine their fate (throw them out, sell them, or decide to watch and read them with all the attendant consequences).

Interactivity is the normal state of every living system, for living means connecting oneself to other systems and reconstructing oneself and others during this connection by means of feedback loops. The unique thing about modernism in the arts was the way it strove to break through this natural state and make systems (works of art) that would not be changed by the uses made of them and that would leave the users completely free to determine how they would be used. Twentieth-century modernism sprang from the fundamental experience that every movement is made up of many still, autonomous moments; the idea was that if one succeeded in creating such a moment, in that moment one could cause both the art and the audience to coincide with themselves, without memories or expectations: only the present would be real. Autonomous art is art that has escaped the interactive order. Autonomous art is "utterly bizarre,"[21] for total alienation offers the only way out of life's insistence that we change things and allow ourselves to be changed: a total disconnection from every feeling, every link to an outside. Modernist art represented nothing but itself, presented nothing but disconnection from itself. The only change it sought to effect in its users was freedom, understood as the experience of nothing.

The main reason that a certain category of art is currently called interactive when in fact everything is interactive is that the public has been trained through long modernist schooling in the interpassive consumption of art: silent reflection on works which give nothing back, in pure white surroundings which do not distract from the numbness brought about by art. Art that explicitly seeks to break through this lethargy, art which does not even exist if the audience does nothing but stand and passively look – for this is what interactive art is – can then indeed be called exceptional. Interactive art is by definition not autonomous or sovereign but designed to have an effect on its audience as well as let that audience affect it. Art that succeeds in getting its audience to bring it into being is easy to distinguish from all the other kinds of art, which try to create an audience for themselves. In sum: interpassive, autonomous art creates an audience; interactive art creates itself via an audience. This can be done digitally but also in other ways. A performance piece, a concert or a play can be interactive with no computers involved.

Every kind of art distinguishes itself from other art forms and from all non-artistic forms by conjuring up a specific kind of illusion which the audience experiences as real. This illusion is the authentic thing in art; it is what legitimizes the art form's existence. It is the reason art invites us to reflect on life, for every illusion art conjures up is a symbolic manifestation of an aspect of our biological existence that can be subjected to reflection only via this symbolic route and not experienced in a direct, non-symbolic way. The word "reflection" does not refer here to either silently losing oneself in a work in order to participate in something beyond words – which was modernism's goal – or postmodernism's critical positioning and simultaneous decontextualization of a work. Instead, reflection is a coming to consciousness in which every human capacity is drawn on and expanded: perception, feeling, intuition, instinct, taste, desire, conscience, self-awareness, memory, imagination, reason. Reflection means expanding one's inner self by looking at (or listening to, touching, smelling or tasting) something external, and deepening one's view of the world by contemplating one's inner self. The insights thus gained can be expressed in words or translated into gestures, practices, worldviews and emotional processes which are embraced rather than avoided. In short, reflection's purpose is – do not be shocked – love.

Susanne K. Langer has called the illusion produced by the various art forms the "virtual object." The virtual object "actualizes" itself in the experience of the viewers, listeners and users of that art; that is, it comes to life in them. Langer has described the virtual object of every form of art known to her, including literature, theater and music as well as the fine arts. Though Langer developed her philosophy during the heyday of modernism, her work neither supports nor apologizes for it: instead she regards modernism as just one way of creating that which is the point of all art in any form, namely "virtual life." Virtual life is life that is actualized by its viewers with the help of the living experiences they carry within themselves. Virtual life has many aspects, spatial as well as temporal, and every art form has appropriated one such aspect. Every art form symbolizes one facet of virtual life. Every art form creates the illusion of being precisely that which it is not, and this illusion is its virtual object.[22]

Painting constructs an illusion of space through the arrangement of shapes and colors on a flat surface. This is the virtual object of painting: a painting's life is in the depth, or apparent space, on the canvas. The virtual object of sculpture is the "kinetic volume" around it: the empty space in which the sculpture seems to move although it is standing still. Architecture creates a virtual "ethnic domain": it makes an arbitrary location into a place that houses a population or a business or a family. Sculpture and architecture are complementary. Virtual kinetic volume is a symbolic representation of the personal space around every individual, and the virtual ethnic domain is a symbolic representation of the shared social environment of which we are all a part. Dance contains virtual forces through which the dancers seem to attract and repel each other, though in reality they can move in almost any direction. The virtual object of music is the controlled, intensified passage of time, of the present, which seems to rhythmically and melodically come to life although the clock keeps ticking as lifelessly as ever.

Novels contain a virtual past; this is why they are (usually) written in the imperfect tense. Novels create the illusion for the reader of getting to know real people in a living past. A novel is a virtual memory constructed in words. The virtual object of the essay is the writer's line of thought which the reader follows as he or she reads – unlike a logically constructed argument, which is correct but not living thought. One might say an essay represents a line of thought rather than being that line of thought (you can be interested in it even if its subject does not concern you). Theater is all about the virtual future: the viewer is not interested in what the characters did in the past, as is the reader of a novel, but only wishes to know what is going to happen to them. Tragedies elaborate on the universal human experience of growing toward a climax, or maturity, after which decline begins and death approaches. In comedies the point is the opposite: that nothing in life ever just ends or peaks in isolation: something else will always happen, unforeseen complications will arise, there will be convergent circumstances or chance meetings too crazy for words.

Every form of art, in short, generates its own kind of illusion of life, of undergoing an experience, of presence, always making one particular aspect of existence accessible to reflection. A work's every aspect, every element, every building block must be an expression of this illusion, this virtual object: art is "living form." Understanding art means understanding what its virtual object is, and understanding which form that object takes in a specific work. An artist's "handwriting," which differentiates her from other artists, consists of the techniques and skills with which she constructs and brings to life the virtual object of a particular art form in her own way.

The reason art exists is that people are filled with experiences and feelings that cannot, or not completely, be translated into language, which is the usual scientific and philosophical instrument for reflection. Painting, sculpture, architecture, music, dance, theater and even poetry, novels and essays concern matters and contain insights which cannot be expressed through logical, consistent argument. The same is true of "technical" art made with cameras, animation, computers, robots, microphones, amplifiers, synthesizers, sensors and other machines. The goal of art is presentational knowledge; that of philosophy and science is discursive knowledge. Discursive knowledge can be articulated, written down, analyzed, abstracted, argued and criticized. Presentational knowledge cannot immediately be captured and described in words, because it is still too new and unfamiliar. It is therefore defined or indicated with the help of images or metaphors: it is shown. Metaphors and presentational images have meaning, but this meaning cannot yet be expressed without their help. "Image" here should be understood as broadly as it is in modern neurology: an image can be a melody, a dance, a building, a poem, an essay, et cetera.

Every art form calls forth a particular kind of presentational knowledge. If you listen to music, whether it is by Händel, Simeon ten Holt, King Sunny Adé or Neil Young, you can tell it "is about something" – you can at least sense that it's "right" or that it sometimes "doesn't work." But what exactly is it about? The answer is that it is about real internal events which take place and are of great importance but which we cannot explain, and yet listening to music we learn much about them. It is about feelings – feelings we recognize but also ones we have never had before. The difference between art and popular culture, in the case of music, is that pop music calls forth feelings in its listeners and lets them wallow in those feelings, while art allows the viewer to recognize, think about and gain insight into them – if not through words then through other feelings, intuition, the universal ability to recognize and explore meaning. Popular culture calls forth sensations; art, reflections. Postmodernist art, in contrast to what is often claimed, strove not to fuse high and low culture but to provoke reflection on the sensations evoked by popular culture.

When we re-view a painting or a building or an installation, or reread a poem, we often find something completely different there than we did the first time. We actualize the virtual dimension of a work of art assisted by previous experiences. This is a significant drawback: often, the older experiences are so strong that they lay themselves over the newly seen or read work and literally make it invisible. If art wishes to evoke a living experience in its audience, then it must play not on specific feelings – the targets of popular culture – but on the universal human capacity to have feelings and to observe them at a distance. Art must make the audience ask: where is this feeling in me coming from? Only then can the viewer, reader or listener genuinely look, read and listen – the second time. There is a moment of delay in art appreciation: art cannot be consumed all at once, in real time, for it never finds its mark before the second encounter, and often it does so only after many confrontations. This necessary delay has long been used as an argument for excluding interactive installations from the sphere of art, for the point of interactive art is almost always immediate reaction (the same as in a computer game: reflect for a second and your avatar will be shot off the screen). But real time is not a necessary precondition for interactive art. Slow interactivity also exists – in buildings, for example, or in landscapes. Influence by and on them can stretch across years, decennia, even centuries.

What is the defining illusion of interactive art? What is the virtual object that is actualized in the visitor or user? What is the presentational image in interactive art that refuses a discursive approach while remaining real, living knowledge? How do we think, or what part of us thinks, when we open ourselves to interactive art? Painting calls forth virtual space by isolating sight from the other senses and calling up an experience of depth solely via the action of the eye (focusing on things at different distances). The visibility of the world, and our seeing of it, thereby become subjects for contemplation: the eye sees itself looking. Sculpture creates a virtual kinetic volume by using a lifeless object to create the space every living body needs around itself to breathe and to move. Around every living person there hangs a cloud of ambiguous clues, sensual or off-putting suggestions and signs of a physical presence that stir associations in us. Sculpture makes this haptic, almost tangible, kinetic volume around the body visible and thus accessible to reflection. The reason statues seem to be alive is that our eyes cannot perceive static forms: if one rests one's gaze on a statue it will soon appear to breathe. Architecture calls forth a virtual ethnic domain by separating one segment of space from the rest of the living environment. Dance evokes virtual forces by showing attraction and repulsion between bodies solely through their movement, which seems to express the dancers' will to go somewhere, imitate others' actions or make variations on them. In this way dance makes visible our habit of ascribing to every behavior a basis in will. But what is will? And what is a living movement? All art takes the trouble and effort to construct something that is spontaneously perceived in daily life, and thereby makes it a subject we can acquire knowledge about, rather than just doing it. Art allows us to enjoy the things that are most familiar to us.

The human faculty that interactive art isolates from all the others is the capacity to react. An interactive work of art contains virtual behavior. By interacting with the work of art we actualize this behavior in ourselves. Interactive art therefore allows us to reflect on what we do naturally without thinking about it, or even being able to. Interactive installations isolate this behavior from everything else in the world. In this sense an installation is comparable to the frame around a painting, the pedestal under a statue, the façade on a building, the paper on which a poem is written. The behavior of the interactive installation visitor is symbolic because it plays out in a vacuum. Every element of the installation – software and hardware, ambiance and interface – must express the virtual behavior that has to be actualized in the visitor to initiate the experience of art and make reflection possible. This reflection is brought about through the way the interactive system reacts to the visitor's behavior. Because the visitor sees, feels or hears what is effected by his or her actions, these actions become the subject of contemplation – sometimes a lightning-fast contemplation, but speed in itself is not a defining characteristic of interactive art. What defines it is the virtual behavior – the behavior of the visitor as well as that of the artwork. An interactive installation ruptures standard behavior and thereby opens the eyes to human and machinic behavioral mechanisms – and it does this for every reaction brought about a second time by the system, every intervention by the user that duplicates itself in the installation.

An animistic conception of objects (including sounds) survives in art, one which dates from mythical prehistory and has never been and never can be displaced by any rational or scientific attitude to life, simply because our senses and brains are finely tuned to detect meaning and traces of life in everything. Meaning is the thing in an object that lives, or has lived and is now dead. But what lives in an object? The virtual feeling that is actualized in us, that comes to life in us (or no longer does, once it is outdated). To live is to feel that we live. Feeling is the basis of all consciousness, including rational thought and the scientific method.[23] Every art object contains a virtual feeling, a feeling given form, which through being given form is virtualized and can thereby be actualized again – if not as experience, then as something it is possible to experience. Works of art, like myths from the animistic phase of human history, are symbols of feelings that must be expressed symbolically for us to be able to get a grip on them, whether to prevent us being overwhelmed by them or to prevent them from slipping away forever. These feelings can be categorized for each art form; see the virtual objects described above.

The feeling that interactivity evokes and makes accessible to reflection is the realization that one does not end at one's skin, that one is more than a body with muscles, a skeleton, sensory organs and a brain: that life means expanding ever further outside oneself, that one's body is always open to influence and that one lives in relation to an outside. This outside is in large part what we are; outside ourselves, we overlap with others, with other living and virtually living systems. Just as to a considerable degree one is one's archive of books, videos, paintings, photo albums, boxes of old letters, diaries, Internet connections. Just as to a considerable degree one is one's mode of transport, whether one drives a car or rides a bicycle. Just as to a considerable degree one is the city one lives in, for it functions like a vast external memory which partly relieves and partly suppresses the internal memory, as one notices when one takes a vacation to the countryside and suddenly recalls various memories one never thinks of at home. People are as intelligent as they are able to make their environments (which is also true of animals), for they are their environments as much as they are themselves.

Like all living creatures, we are distributed cognitive systems, distributed memory systems, action systems and emotional systems. Our feelings distribute themselves in the form of virtual experiences which we localize in objects, people and places. This is why we avoid certain streets or neighborhoods, why we sit next to certain people and not others on trains and in waiting rooms, why we find some restaurants pleasant and not others, feel comfortable with some neighbors and not others, and so on. This whole cloud of intangible feelings and parts of us experienced outside ourselves is what interactive art explores and lays open to reflection. Interactive art helps us to understand why we react to things as we do, and why the outside world reacts the way it does. Interactivity designers "design" virtual behavior so that users do not have to think about it (unless there is an error in the system): virtual behavior is actualized transparently and unconsciously. Interactivity artists make actualization hypermedial: they allow virtual behavior to design itself, develop itself to such a degree that its users experience all its incomprehensibility and thereby learn to consciously deploy it, with the goal of making it something we share with others because we allow others to create it, just as we create their behavior. The goal – do not be shocked – is mutual love.

# From Media to Software Theory

The computer, so goes an oft-repeated proposition, remediates all preceding media – look around on a few websites and you will find not
only written and printed texts, photographs, film and video, television,
and security cameras (webcams), but also scanned paintings, drawings,
etchings and so on. Through computer speakers one can listen to LPs,
CDs, MP3s, radio programs and film scores. One can send letters by
email, and even telephone through the 'net. Once all media were moved
to digital carriers, the computer became a metamedium, a repository in
which a user can jump from medium to medium with the click of a
mouse. But this is not so much a remediation of all old and new media
as a hybridization, a merging of different kinds of media into a new
entity. This unity is symbolized by the laptop, in which all media are
brought together and become mobile, portable, playable and usable
everywhere. How do the various media bear up under this hybridization? Can the separate elements still be recognized on the basis of their
historic origins, or has something new been created? And to understand
it, is a knowledge of history unnecessary, perhaps even a hindrance? An
earlier example of the hybridization of two media shows us how much
"monomedia" change in such a merging.

One remarkable but little-noticed aspect of sound film is that
viewers remember virtually all information conveyed through the audio
channel (the soundtrack) as if it had been conveyed through the pictures. Moreover, if the "audiovisual illusion" is functioning correctly, the
viewers will be silently convinced that the pictures contain all the
important information and the sound only duplicates it – even when it
is really the sound that is generating the meaning. As has already been
mentioned, in speech practically all meaning is conveyed through the
intonation and timbre of the voice, emphases on certain words, pauses,
hesitations and the rhythm of speech and silence, supplemented by the
nonverbal signals we send out with facial expressions, gestures and
general posture – even though this meaning seems to be established in
the words and sentences we say. Silent film took advantage of the fact
that we often speak with our whole bodies: even without voices it was
easy to tell what the actors were talking about. Sound film – or "talking pictures" – allowed them to transmit most of their meaning through
the voice, making expression and gesticulation less important. After
twenty years of sound film, actors like Marlon Brando and James Dean
were mumbling unintelligibly instead of bothering to articulate proper-
ly: the drift of what they were saying came across anyway.

We process sound so naturally that it is difficult for us to become conscious of its influence. We also perceive vastly more sound than we do visual input: humans can distinguish only twenty images per second (as opposed to, for example, carrier pigeons, which can see 150), but we perceive and process many more sounds than that. With practice, we can learn to hear extremely fast sequences of sounds, but it is impossible for us to learn to see equally fast series of images. Our ease of hearing is the true reason why it is so frequently said that we live in a "visual culture," but the increase in the number of images over the past century is insignificant compared with the rise of sound levels in the city and countryside. Sound is the blind spot of visual culture, beginning with film. Cinematic sound, for instance film music (a remediation of opera), can impart a convincing coherence to an unrelated series of images. The music connects the images across the breaks caused by editing, as can be done with the sound of an approaching car or a rising storm and so on. Sound is the most important means filmmakers have for creating a sense of the space outside the frame. Thus cinematic sound affects the experience of time – the progress of time between edited images – as well as of space outside and inside the frame. When we see two actors walking out of the distance, and hear their voices the whole time as if they are directly in front of the camera, we experience this as something totally natural. In cinema there is an "audiovisual contract," a tacit agreement between sound and image whereby the sound influences what we see and conversely the picture determines what we hear consciously or unconsciously.[24] Something similar happens in "visual culture": the muzak in shopping malls guides the eye as if automatically toward the merchandise (and we stop noticing the music), and the racket in the street determines how we navigate through the traffic, without us really even having to see the other road users (while conversely we have so many visual impressions to process that the noise of the road does not crush us).

Sound in films almost never has a power of its own; it virtually always exists to serve the images. Let us take film music as an example. It can be used "empathetically," to provide a direct interpretation of the feeling expressed in the accompanying scene. But music can also be deployed "unempathetically": in such cases, it is clearly indifferent to what is happening in the picture. The surprising effect of the latter is that what the viewer sees becomes highly emotionally charged, as, for example, when the music comes from a jukebox or a dance band that plays on as a silent emotional storm takes place for the protagonists. Empathetic, interpretive music renders the film and its emotions transparent; unempathetic, indifferent music makes them hypermedial, outstandingly cinematic and thereby that much more gripping. Note that what is described here holds true for single scenes, never entire films (though there are other means of achieving transparency and hypermediation besides soundtrack).

Because of their linear arrangement, cinematic images always tell a story, a sequence of events ordered chronologically and causally. But there is no such thing as a soundtrack that is similarly ordered. When we hear a soundtrack without the picture, what we hear is not a story but disparate sounds that sometimes acquire a coherence but then fall apart again. Coherence is sometimes created in film music through the use of a leitmotif for each character, but soundtracks never achieve the consistency of opera. But sound does impose a chronology on the pictures: in silent films often scenes were shown one after the other with the expectation that the viewers would understand that they were occurring simultaneously. This is not possible in sound film, for synchronous sound always progresses chronologically and thus forces the images to move in a "natural" sequence. Nor do sounds logically follow from each other in film, while events in a film usually do happen causally: city noises can be immediately followed by violin music while the same urban scene remains on screen. Unlike cinematic images, film sounds can come from multiple sources and be mixed into one seemingly natural soundscape. Only with the invention of digital techniques did it become possible to lay images from different sources – visual fragments, artificial images, animation, decelerated and accelerated footage – over each other and combine them seamlessly into one new, apparently natural picture. The digital film image has acquired the status that sound in film always had: it looks convincing, does not focus attention on itself, and influences the farthest reaches of the viewer's emotional experience.

Image and sound in film cannot easily be told apart, even with plenty of practice. Viewers think that they have seen things they have only heard, or that they have heard actors speaking when only music was audible. No memory is as unreliable as the memory of a movie scene that once made a strong impression. When one sees a favorite old film years later, events in it are usually very different from the pictures one has in one's mind and that have perhaps had a deep influence on one's life. Sometimes we seem to remember sounds as images and images as sounds. In everyday life, intense feelings often cannot be regenerated by an image alone – for example, the memory of a person one was head-over-heels in love with ten years earlier, of whom one has only a meaningless photograph in a desk drawer. But then one unexpectedly hears the music that was always playing back then and the tears trickle down one's face: We were so happy then! To say that sound film is a remediation of silent film combined with older sound carriers like the wax cylinder and the phonograph is somewhat superficial. The optical soundtrack was already unprecedented in the history of sound recording: sound photographed. And the film reel, a series of transparent photographs projected on a screen with a strong lamp to create the impression of movement, was equally novel. Silent film was not a remediation of the magic lantern (an early projection device). A photograph is a small surface one can hold in one's hand; a cinematic picture is so large that it seems to move directly in the mind of the viewer. The combination of sound and motion picture was something astonishingly new, a hybridization and mutual contamination of the visible and the audible making up a single total experience which was unique. Digital film later remediated and expanded this experience.

Television is another example of a medium that is mainly supposed to remediate older media but has become something completely different. We can, of course, see films, documentaries, plays, videos, photographs, illustrated radio programs and telephone conversations on television. But we view all these remediated "media" differently on television than we do in their original settings. Many media are reproduced on the screen, but one cannot look to these media to understand television, however heavily TV refers to them. A typical televisual form such as the news differentiates itself from the medium of video by means of live reports, which are designed to prove that there has been too little time to manipulate the image. Live broadcasts guarantee the cinematic truth of what we see, though it is not a film since film is never live. Other televisual forms such as soaps and sitcoms are definitely not film either, although they are made according to the cinematic process: manipulation happens at the level of editing and not – or rarely – at the level of the image. The difference between a series and a film is that one must watch a film from beginning to end to understand it, but one can start watching a television series at any point in any episode. A series is not a film in serial form: series consist of chains of ideas which neither drive each other nor cancel each other out, as they would in a movie, but merely alternate. The suspense of television lies in seeing what the next link will look like. Who did what in previous episodes is not important. The ideas speak for themselves.

On television one watches programs: that is, one follows the programs the characters act out. These can be banal – programs of grouchy fathers and quiz contestants – or refined and complex – ones of metaphysically inclined special agents and confessed gambling addicts. TV programs are often dependent on a situation: a wedding, a competition, a prison, a police station or a news situation such as a plane crash or a political conflict. The only reality depicted in the television image is that of the programs of the characters and the situations they find themselves in. Television does not show who they are, where they are going or who they will become, as photography, film and video do. Every TV episode, whether it is of a soap or a current affairs show, shows in an instructive manner how programs function somewhere and how they affect each other. We watch out of curiosity to see what inventions a well-known program will come up with next. A program tells us *how*: how one can hold one's own in a particular environment. Television is not good at telling us *why*: why would one want to hold one's own? That is more of a task for literature and the movies. There are no people to be seen on television: we see only the conceptual structures within which they move. This allows the television image to be totally transparent and understandable while always keeping a distance and remaining strange. Television can at once bore us and fascinate us.

The purpose of television is that the viewer can enter any imaginable program at any moment: as a fashion model or a mother, an artist or a manager, a child or a senior citizen. Anyone can make a television program their own, while not everyone can become a film or pop star. And yet film stars on TV are nothing more than programs themselves, whether they are acting in movies or appearing on talk shows. On talk shows they perform the movie star program; in films shown on TV, the actor program. The same is true of pop stars who appear in videos and interviews. If you are going to appear on television, you should ask yourself: which program should I make of myself, and how? Show how you do whatever it is you have been invited to be on TV for, and make immediately clear by means of a tormented or sympathetic expression that there is something behind it (you need not explain what). The fact that every TV season, as exceptions to prove the rule, there are one or two series about "real people" (as real, that is, as the actors in a good movie), as opposed to programs, caricatures and stereotypes, demonstrates that the present state of affairs is not really so bad. Too much reality would make television an unbearable medium, one you could watch for an hour a week at most. Documentary photography, which depicts a misery the viewer always knows has really taken place or is still going on, becomes depressing if you look at too much of it. If the audience wishes to engage enjoyably with a medium, a healthy dose of silliness is called for.

Another medial sphere in which the influence of hybridization is much greater than that of remediation is music. Nowadays, people train themselves, starting in childhood, to process large numbers of impressions simultaneously. This is one reason why young people's bars are so noisy – "learn to deal with it" is the ethic. It is also one reason drugs are so popular, for practically all drugs provide a chemical filter that lets in some impressions and not others: the user loses contact with a large part of his or her environment but at the same time learns to concentrate on an essential bandwidth within the stream of incoming information. Every new kind of music contains so many unfamiliar rhythms, melodies, tonalities, counterpoints, lyrics and noise – or else manages to omit them – that lovers of older musical forms do not know what to make of it. It's ugly, you can't dance to it, it's unsingable, it's screaming or squeaky or droning, it makes no sense, it's inhuman, et cetera. This judgment has been visited upon rock, pop, disco, dance, trance, hip-hop, trip-hop, glitch and so on. New music contains so much information that one would rather not listen to it. Inventing or developing a new rhythm is difficult, and yet people manage to do it again and again, and the newest rhythms are always bizarre, obscure, complicated, one moment made up of many older rhythms and the next breaking away from them entirely. The inventor of a new rhythm invents a new way of moving, and thus a new way of experiencing the world.[25] Rhythms, pulsating beats, are a ideal way to process torrents of information. They filter and amplify very specifically; like drugs, they make the world new for a while. The point of media use is not to remediate something old into something new or to make something new reappear in something old, but to allow the old and the new to hybridize into something unprecedented, and then go a step further so that one must reorganize one's whole internal order in order to process the information streams, thereby becoming something unique and characteristic of oneself and the generation one is a part of.

This brings us back to computers, and to the practice of emulation. Emulation is the translation of hardware into software. Emulation makes it possible to run not only every old and yet-to-be-developed PC program on the average computer, but also every version of Apple and Atari and their applications; everything for PlayStation, Nintendo, Vectrex, Gameboy; and the arcade and slot machine programs of the past, present and future – in short, all the hardware of every time and everything it ever was, is and will be capable of doing. The entire digital universe is made up of ones and zeros, and can therefore theoretically be called forth on a single machine. The fact that there are different types of hardware is an expression of the economic boundaries between the different computer makers. These economic boundaries are a consequence not of the traits of the computer medium but of historical circumstances – from designers' ambitions to business people's need to earn money. Emulation is the translation of this accidental digital segmentation back into one universal code that can run on any hardware. Emulation ruptures the artificial boundaries between hard- and software companies and thereby wipes out the economic and cultural history of the computer medium. Paradoxically enough, emulation is at the same time the only means computers have of safeguarding and unlocking their own history, what with one antique format after the other being lost. Emulating all the hardware and software of the past is the only way computer history can be written on the computer itself. Social and financial reality outside the computer do not appear in this version of history, but everything computers themselves were ever capable of does. In emulating games, the post-historical generation of computer fans can preserve all its past trances, now and forever. And this answers the question of whether the computer is something totally new or just a collection of remediated older media.

If it is true that even a computer's hardware can be converted into software, and all other "media" remediated on computers are nothing more than software packages, then there is no longer any point in speaking of media when we talk about computers. Nor does "new media" make sense, even if the word "media" is used in the singular despite being a plural form. Anyone wishing to thoroughly understand the digital universe need not try to discover what exactly is new about various applications, and which of their functions have existed before in analog form: the language of new media is written not in words or pictures but in zeros and ones.[26] Looking around the computers' digital universe, one sees hardware, software, networks, objects, environments, situations, and spaces, but no media – for everything there communicates, and when everything is a means of communication, the word "medium" loses its explanatory power. In the digital sphere, everything ultimately is or can be converted into software. History, too, is software – a network of databases along with a series of search engines. What the computer age needs is a unified software theory. That is beyond the reach of media theory.

204

Notes

## Preface
1. Marchand 1989/1998; Gordon 1977.
2. Cassirer 1955–1957.

## Media Theory: The New Science
1. Vico 1725/1999.
2. Damasio 2003.
3. Mulder 1996.
4. Wolfram 2002; Fredkin 2003.
5. McLuhan and McLuhan 1988.
6. Bateson 1979.
7. McLuhan 1964.
8. Gleick 2003.
9. Langer 1942.

## General Media Theory
1. Shannon and Weaver 1949.
2. Wiener 1954.
3. Bateson 1973.
4. Maturana and Varela 1998.
5. Damasio 1999.
6. Brooks 2002.
7. Flusser 2002.
8. Virilio 1986, 1991, 1999, 1999, and 2004.
9. Baudrillard 1990.
10. Enzensberger 1991.
11. Appadurai 1996.
12. West 1939.
13. Warhol 1975.
14. Varela, Thompson and Rosch 1993.
15. Langer 1953.
16. Bolter and Grusin 1999.
17. Bazin 1971. Barthes 1993.
18. Benjamin 1969.
19. Gibson 1984, 1986 and 1989.
20. Adilkno 1998.
21. Canetti 1981.
22. Debord 1995.
23. Lyotard 1984.
24. Mulder 2000.
25. Groys 2000.

## Historical Media Theory
1. Whitehead 1927.
2. Burckhardt 1979.

3. Smith 1776.
4. Marx and Engels 1998.
5. Foucault 1990.
6. Innis 1951.
7. McLuhan 1968.
8. Tylor 1871.
9. McLuhan 1968.
10. Herder 1996.
11. Burroughs 1981.
12. Cassirer 1944, 1946 and 1946.
13. Graves 1948.
14. Lévi-Strauss 1966.
15. Langer 1942.
16. Duerr 1988.
17. Langer 1953.
18. Linke 2000.
19. Pound 1970.
20. Lord 1960/2000.
21. Goody 1986 and 1987.
22. Havelock 1963/1967.
23. Morris 2003.
24. Olson 1994.
25. Schmandt-Besserat 1996.
26. Ong 1982.
27. Havelock 1986.
28. Gerard Bricogne, in: Buchanan 2002.
29. McLuhan 1962.
30. Alpers 1983.
31. Eisenstein 1983.
32. Freund 1980.
33. Lemaire 1970.
34. Baudrillard 1993 and 1996.
35. Kittler 1999.
36. Theweleit 1987/1989.
37. Williams 1961.
38. Ong 1971.
39. Peters 1999.
40. Ronell 1989.
41. McLuhan 1964.
42. Virilio 2004.
43. Plant 2003.
44. Ong 1977 and 1982.
45. Baudrillard 1990.
46. Mulder 2002.
47. Theweleit 1994.
48. Flusser 1993.
49. Kittler 1992.
50. Bliven 1954.

51. Theweleit 1988.
52. Singh 1999.
53. Turing 1936/1965.
54. Joyce 1987.
55. Bolter 1989/2001.
56. Hayles 2002.
57. Oosterhoff 2002.
58. Lovink 2002 and 2003.
59. Gleick 1988.
60. Hayles 1999.

## Practical Media Theory

1. Adilkno 1994.
2. Debord 1995.
3. McLuhan 1970.
4. Marcus 1989.
5. Plant 1992.
6. Bey 1991.
7. Burroughs and Gysin 1979. See also: Kuri 2003.
8. Burroughs 1971/1979.
9. Home 1991.
10. Metzger 1996.
11. Groys 1992.
12. Hayles 2002.
13. O'Doherty 1999.
14. Adilkno 1998.
15. Mulder 2000.
16. Lilly 1974.
17. Mulder 1996.
18. Duncan 1977.
19. McLuhan 1999.
20. Pfaller 2000.
21. Charles Baudelaire, in: Baudrillard 1990.
22. Langer 1953.
23. Damasio 1994.
24. Chion 1994.
25. Eshun 1998.
26. Manovich 2001.

# Bibliography

*The titles starred compose a selective reading list in media theory.*

Adilkno, *Cracking the Movement: Squatting beyond the Media*, New York 1994.
* –, *Media Archive, World Edition*, New York 1998.
Alpers, Svetlana, *The Art of Describing: Dutch Art in the Seventeenth Century*, Chicago 1983.
Appadurai, Arjun, *Modernity at Large*, New York 1996.
Barthes, Roland, *Camera Lucida: Reflections on Photography*, London 1993.
Bateson, Gregory, *Steps to an Ecology of Mind*, London 1973.
–, *Mind and Nature, A Necessary Unity*, New York 1979.
Baudrillard, Jean, *Fatal Strategies*, New York 1990.
–, *Symbolic Exchange and Death*, London 1993.
–, *The Perfect Crime*, London 1996.
Bazin, André, *What is Cinema*, Berkeley 1971.
* Benjamin, Walter, "The Work of Art in the Age of Mechanical Reproduction" in: *Illuminations*, New York 1969.
Bey, Hakim, *The Temporary Autonomous Zone*, New York 1991.
Bliven Jr, Bruce, *The Wonderful Writing Machine*, New York 1954.
Bolter, Jay David, *Turing's Man: Western Culture in the Computer Age*, New York 1984.
–, *Writing Space: The Computer in the History of Literacy*, Hillsdale (NJ) 1989. Rewritten version: *Writing Space: Computers, Hypertext, and the Remediation of Print*, Mahwah (NJ) 2001.
* –, and Richard Grusin, *Remediation: Understanding New Media*, London 1999.
–, and Diane Gromala, *Windows and Mirror: Interaction Design, Digital Art, and the Myth of Transparency*, Cambridge (Mass.) 2003.
Brooks, Rodney, *Flesh and Machines*, Cambridge (Mass.) 2002.
Buchanan, Mark, *Small World: Uncovering Nature's Hidden Networks*, New York 2002.
Burckhardt, Jacob, *Reflections on History*, Indianapolis 1979.
Burroughs, William S., "The Electronic Revolution" in: *The Job*, New York 1971. Reprinted in: *Ah Pook is Here*, London 1979.
–, *Cities of the Red Night*, London 1981.
–, *The Adding Machine*, London 1985.
–, and Brion Gysin, *The Third Mind*, London 1979.
Canetti, Elias, *Crowds and Power*, New York 1981.
Cassirer, Ernst, *An Essay on Man*, New Haven 1944.

\* —, *Myth and Language*, New York 1946.

—, *The Myth of the State*, New Haven 1946.

—, *The Philosophy of Symbolic Forms* (Volume 1: *Language*, Volume 2: *Mythical Thought*, Volume 3: *The Phenomenology of Knowledge*), New Haven 1955–1957.

\* Chion, Michel, *Audio-Vision: Sound on Screen*, New York 1994.

Damasio, Antonio, *Descartes' Error*, New York 1994.

—, *The Feeling of What Happens*, New York 1999.

—, *Looking for Spinoza*, New York 2003.

Debord, Guy, *The Society of the Spectacle*, New York 1995.

Duerr, Hans-Peter, *Nacktheit und Scham: Der Mythos vom Zivilisationsprozess* (Nudity and shame: the myth of the civilization process), Frankfurt 1988.

Duncan, Isadora, *The Art of the Dance* (Introduction Sheldon Cheney), New York 1977.

Eisenstein, Elizabeth L., *The Printing Revolution in Early Modern Europe*, Cambridge 1983.

Enzensberger, Hans Magnus, "Das Nullmedium oder Warum alle Klagen über das Fernsehen gegenstandslos sei" in: *Mittelmaß und Wahn: Gesammelte Zerstreuungen* (The zero medium, or why it doesn't make sense to complain about television, in: Mediocrity and delusion), Frankfurt 1991.

Eshun, Kodwo, *More Brilliant Than the Sun: Adventures in Sonic Fiction*, London 1998.

Flusser, Vilém, *Nachgeschichte: Eine korrigierte Geschichtsschreibung* (Posthistory: a rewriting of history), Bensheim and Dusseldorf 1993.

\* —, *Writings*, Minneapolis 2002.

Foucault, Michel, *The History of Sexuality – Volume I: An Introduction*, New York 1990.

Freund, Gisèle, *Photography & Society*, London 1980.

Fredkin, Edward, *Introduction to Digital Philosophy*, Internet 2003.

Gibson, William, *Neuromancer*, New York 1984.

—, *Count Zero*, New York 1986.

—, *Mona Lisa Overdrive*, New York 1989.

Gleick, James, *Chaos: Making a New Science*, New York 1988.

—, *Isaac Newton*, New York 2003.

Goody, Jack, *The Domestication of the Savage Mind*, Cambridge 1977.

—, *The Logic of Writing and the Organization of Society*, Cambridge 1986.

—, *The Interface Between the Written and the Oral*, Cambridge 1987.

Gordon, W. Terrence, *Marshall McLuhan: Escape into Understanding*, New York 1977.

Graves, Robert, *The White Goddess*, London 1948.

Groys, Boris, *Über das Neue: Versuch einer Kulturökonomie* (About the new: attempt at an economy of culture), Munich 1992.

\* –, *Unter Verdacht* (Under suspicion), Munich 2000.

\* Havelock, Eric A., *Preface to Plato*, New York 1963/1967.

–, *The Muse Learns to Write*, New Haven 1986.

Hayles, N. Katherine, *How We Became Posthuman: Virtual Bodies in Cybernetics, Literature, and Informatics*, Chicago and London 1999.

\* –, *Writing Machines*, Cambridge (Mass.) 2002.

Herder, Johann Gottfried, *On the Origin of Language*, Chicago 1996.

Home, Stewart, *The Art Strike Papers and Neoist Manifestos: The Years without Art, 1990–1993*, Edinburgh 1991.

\* Innis, Harold, *The Bias of Communication*, Toronto 1951.

Joyce, Michael, *Afternoon, a story*, Watertown 1987.

Kittler, Friedrich, *Discourse Networks 1800/1900*, Stanford 1992.

–, *Gramophone, Film, Typewriter*, Stanford 1999.

Kuri, José Férez (ed.), *Brion Gysin: Tuning into the Multimedia Age*, London 2003.

Langer, Susanne K., *Philosophy in a New Key*, New York 1942.

\* –, *Feeling and Form*, London 1953.

Lash, Scott, *Critique of Information*, London 2002.

Lemaire, Ton, *Filosofie van het landschap* (Landscape philosophy), Baarn 1970.

Lévi-Strauss, Claude, *The Savage Mind*, Chicago 1966.

Lilly, John C., *The Human Biocomputer: Theory and Experiments*, London 1974.

Linke, Detlef, "The Rhythms of Happiness," in: Joke Brouwer (ed.), *Machine Times*, Rotterdam 2000.

\* Lord, Albert B., *The Singer of Tales*, Cambridge (Mass.) 1960/2000.

Lovink, Geert, *Dark Fiber: Tracking Critical Internet Culture*, Cambridge (Mass.) 2002.

–, *My First Recession: Critical Internet Culture in Transition*, Rotterdam 2003.

Lyotard, Jean-François, *The Postmodern Condition*, Minneapolis 1984.

\* Manovich, Lev, *The Language of New Media*, Cambridge (Mass.) 2001.

Marchand, Philip, *Marshall McLuhan: The Medium and the Messenger*, Cambridge (Mass.) 1989 and 1998.

Marcus, Greil, *Lipstick Traces: A Secret History of the Twentieth Century*, London 1989.

Marx, Karl, and Friedrich Engels, *The Communist Manifesto*, Oxford 1998.

Maturana, Humberto R., and Francisco J. Varela, *The Tree of Knowledge: The Biological Roots of Human Understanding* (revised edition), Boston and London 1998.

* McLuhan, Marshall, *The Gutenberg Galaxy: The Making of Typographic Man*, Toronto 1962.

* —, *Understanding Media*, New York 1964.

* —, *The Medium is the Massage*, New York 1968.

—, *War and Peace in the Global Village*, New York 1968.

—, *Counterblast*, London 1970.

—, *The Medium and the Light*, Totonto 1999.

—, and Eric McLuhan, *Laws of Media: The New Science*, Toronto 1988.

Metzger, Gustav, "Earth to Galaxies: On Destruction and Destructivity," lecture in Glasgow 1996.

Morris, Simon Conway, *Life's Solution*, Cambridge 2003.

Mulder, Arjen, *Het twintigste-eeuwse lichaam* (The twentieth-century body), Amsterdam 1996.

—, *Het fotografisch genoegen* (The photographic enjoyment), Amsterdam 2000.

—, *Levende systemen: Reis naar het einde van het informatietijdperk* (Living systems: journey to the end of the information age), Amsterdam 2002.

—, and Maaike Post, *Book for the Electronic Arts*, Rotterdam 2000.

O'Doherty, Brian, *Inside the White Cube: The Ideology of the Gallery Space* (expanded edition), Berkeley 1999.

* Olson, David R., *The World on Paper*, Cambridge 1994.

Ong, Walter J., *Rhetoric, Romance, and Technology*, Ithaca and London 1971.

—, *Interfaces of the Word*, Ithaca and London 1977.

—, *Orality and Literacy: The Technologizing of the Word*, London 1982.

Oosterhoff, Tonnus, *Wij zagen ons in een kleine groep mensen veranderen* (We noticed being changed into a small group of people), Amsterdam 2002.

Peters, John Durham, *Speaking into the Air: A History of the Idea of Communication*, Chicago and London 1999.

Pfaller, Robert, *Interpassivität: Studien über delegiertes Genießen* (Interpassivity: studies about delegated pleasure), Vienna 2000.

Plant, Sadie, *The Most Radical Gesture: The Situationist International in a Postmodern Age*, London 1992.

–, *Zeros + Ones: Digital Women + the New Technoculture*, New York 1997.

–, "Mobile Knitting" in: Joke Brouwer and Arjen Mulder (ed.), *Information is Alive*, Rotterdam 2003.

Pound, Ezra, *Jefferson and/or Mussolini*, New York 1970.

Ronell, Avital, *The Telephone Book: Technology, Schizophrenia, Electric Speech*, Lincoln and London 1989.

* Schmandt-Besserat, Denise, *How Writing Came About*, Austin 1996.

* Shannon, Claude E., and Warren Weaver, *The Mathematical Theory of Communication*, Urbana 1949.

Singh, Simon, *The Code Book*, London 1999.

Smith, Adam, *An Inquiry into the Nature and Causes of the Wealth of Nations*, London 1776.

Snell, Bruno, *The Discovery of the Mind in Greek Philosophy and Literature*, New York 1960.

Theweleit, Klaus, *Male Phantasies I and II,* Mineapolis 1987 and 1989.

–, *Buch der Könige 1: Orpheus ~~und~~ Euridike* (Book of kings: Orpheus and Eurydice), Basel and Frankfurt 1988.

–, *Buch der Könige 2: Orpheus am Machtpol* (Book of kings: Orpheus at the power pole), Basel and Frankfurt 1994.

Turing, Alan, "On Computable Numbers, with an Application to the Entscheidungsproblem" (1936), in: Martin Davis (ed.), *Undecidable: Basic Papers on Problems Propositions, Unsolvable Problems and Computable Functions*, New York 1965.

Tylor, Edward B., *Primitive Culture*, London 1871.

Varela, Francisco J., Evan Thompson and Eleanor Rosch, *The Embodied Mind*, Cambridge (Mass.) 1993.

Vico, Giambattista, *New Science* (*Principii di una scienza nuova d'i-torno alla natura delle nazioni*, Naples 1725), London 1999.

Virilio, Paul, *Speed and Politics*, New York 1986.

–, *Lost Dimension,* New York 1991.

–, *Polar Inertia,* London 1999.

–, *Open Sky*, London 1999.

–, *Negative Horizon*, London 2004.

Warhol, Andy, *From A to B and Back Again*, New York 1975.

West, Nathaniel, *The Day of the Locusts*, New York 1939.

Whitehead, Alfred North, *Symbolism: Its Meaning and Effect*, New York 1927.

Wiener, Norbert, *The Human Use of Human Beings*, New York 1954.
Williams, Raymond, *The Long Revolution*, London 1961.
—, *Britain in the Sixties: Communications*, Harmondsworth 1962.
Wolfram, Stephen, *A New Kind of Science*, Champaign (IL) 2002.

# Acknowlegdment

In writing the first and third parts of this book I have drawn on earlier books and articles of mine, some of which appeared under my own name and some of which I wrote with others under the name of Adilkno (Foundation for the Advancement of Illegal Knowledge). I list the original titles in the Bibliography. All the pieces used here have been adapted and further developed, in part because I have become more deeply acquainted with media theory over the years, and in part because, unlike the source texts, the present book makes no literary pretensions. I have used the same selection criteria for my own publications as I have for media theory works by other people: I have (re)used only the parts that have stood up over the many classes, guest lectures, readings, workshops and courses I have given in a wide range of places. I wish to thank my students, listeners and questioners, and those who walked out of my lectures, for their contribution to my improved grasp of the weak and strong points of media theory, and of my media theory in particular. I also thank the editors of my earlier books and articles for their comments, suggestions and encouragements. Finally, I thank Joke Brouwer, who made it possible for me to write and publish this book; Laura Martz, who translated the book into English so rigorously; and Maaike Post, coauthor of *Book for the Electronic Arts* and of my life, for her help in realizing this book and for her strict but fair editing of the final text.

Production and design: Joke Brouwer

This book was made possible by the financial support of the VSBfonds, the
Netherlands.

Available in North, South and Central America through
D.A.P./Distributed Art Publishers Inc, 155 Sixth Avenue 2nd Floor,
New York, NY 10013-1507, Tel 212 6271999, Fax 212 6279484.

Available in the United Kingdom and Ireland through Art Data,
12 Bell Industrial Estate, 50 Cunnington Street, London W4 5HB,
Tel 208 7471061, Fax 208 7422319.

Printed and bound in the Netherlands

ISBN 90-5662-388-5

Other books published by V2_: http://publishing.v2.nl